UNDERSTANDING Pittsburgh

Guide for International Visitors and Residents

D0733497

Pittsburgh Council for International Visitors

Table of Contents

Acknowledgements

Understanding Pittsburgh: A Guide for International Visitors and Residents received generous support from the Fisher Fund of The Pittsburgh Foundation and the Heinz Endowments.

Dr. Joanne F. White, a former member of the PCIV Board of Directors with expatriate experience in Germany, assisted in the intial development of the project.

This guide was researched and written by the staff and associates of Echo International (formerly known as The Language Center, Inc.). PCIV extends its deepest thanks to staff members Alan Isaac and David Holzer. Les Dutka, President, was instrumental in the planning and structure of the guide as well as in the selection of writing, editing, and creative resources.

Gail Shrott, Executive Director of the Pittsburgh Council for International Visitors provided invaluable assistance in identifying topics to be included in the guide, editing of text, and critical oversight.

Masami Orihara of Japan reviewed the guide's content and contributed her insights.

The map on page vii is from *Pittsburgh: An Urban Portrait*, by Franklin Toker, ©1986. Reprinted by permission of the University of Pittsburgh Press.

PCIV is grateful to the Greater Pittsburgh Covention & Visitors Bureau for their cooperation in supplying the maps accompanying this publication.

Additionally, we would like thank the Western Pennsylvania Conservancy/ Fallingwater for the use of their photo on page 105.

Foreword

Welcome to Pittsburgh

This guide has been designed to help you feel at home in Pittsburgh, whether you will live here for a short time or for many years. The Pittsburgh Council for International Visitors (PCIV), in collaboration with The Language Center, Inc., has created this guide to provide you with information that will help you adapt to life in our city.

PCIV is a community-based non-profit organization that was founded in 1959. The mission of the organization is to promote cultural, educational, and commercial ties among Western Pennsylvanians and other peoples of the world. Through personal interaction, the organization facilitates the forging of friendships and professional relationships. PCIV is a valuable resource for international visitors living in the Pittsburgh community.

Since its founding, PCIV volunteers have worked with international visitors and their families to ease their transition to life in Pittsburgh. Plans for this guide grew directly out of a 1991 PCIV-sponsored study of the social support services needed by Pittsburgh's international residents. That study was conducted by Duquesne University. It identified spouses' concerns with language, schools, and participation in a foreign culture. As international companies invest in our region and local companies expand into international markets, Pittsburgh has much to offer to international visitors.

We encourage you to use this guide as your first step in discovering Pittsburgh. This guide includes references to other valuable sources of information. Our doors are open to you. Welcome.

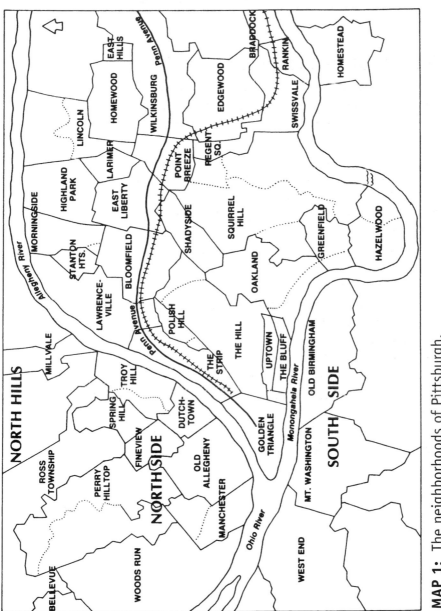

MAP 1: The neighborhoods of Pittsburgh.

1 Background

World-Class Business City

Pittsburghers, especially native Pittsburghers, are proud of their city. Given the opportunity, they will tell you so. There are many self-promoting books, magazines, videos, and programs that present Pittsburgh in the best possible way. Pittsburgh pride is justified. The city has become a booming center for high technology industry and a magnet for foreign corporations. This might be the reason that you are reading this now!

According to the Greater Pittsburgh Convention and Visitors Bureau (1997) "Over 800 firms and 800,000 employees are involved in Pittsburgh's Advanced Technology industries." With 350 software firms located here, this city is ranked tenth in the nation in U.S. software employment. Carnegie Mellon University is considered one of the best institutions for software engineering in the United States.

Robotics is a growing area to which Pittsburghers point with special pride; NASA Robotics, RedZone Robotics, and the Engineering Consortium are based in Pittsburgh. Some of the fastest growing telecommunication companies—Fore Systems, Tollgrade Communications, Black Box Corporation, Computerm, and ITS—are located here.

There are, according to the *Pittsburgh Business Times*, more than 150 foreign companies in Western Pennsylvania, including 62 from Germany, 27 from Great Britain, 14 from Canada, and 12 from Japan. Other countries with firms in the area include Australia, Austria, Brazil, Czech Republic, Israel, Korea, and Sweden. Pittsburgh is also headquarters to many Fortune 500 companies, including USX Corporation, Alcoa, H.J. Heinz Company, PPG Industries, Inc., PNC Bank, Mellon Bank, Allegheny Teledyne Inc., and CNG.

What accounts for this remarkable convergence of talent, energy, and resources? Pittsburgh has a convenient central geographic location with access to over 50% of U.S. and Canadian markets, an excellent standard of living at relatively low cost, and a trained and willing labor force with a strong work ethic. The crime rate is low; according to Penn's Southwest Association, the Pittsburgh metropolitan area has the lowest crime rate for any metropolitan area with over one million people. More statistics are in Chapter 14. Our city has all of these advantages, and more.

City of Neighborhoods

In the United States, most cities and their surrounding suburbs are becoming more similar to each other due to the spread of chain stores, chain restaurants, shopping centers, and housing communities built with cars in mind. However, it is worth looking for the intangibles that make a city unique and truly enjoyable. Here are some general observations about Pittsburgh to give you an insider's view of the city.

Pittsburgh is a city of people, neighborhoods, hills, rivers, and changing seasons. Pittsburghers are friendly and hardworking. They are proud and supportive of the local professional sports teams, the Steelers (American football), the Pirates (baseball), and the Penguins (ice hockey). People tend to identify with their neighborhoods.

Pittsburgh has about 90 distinct neighborhoods, each with its own character. Here are a few neighborhood profiles:

- **Oakland** is the neighborhood where the University of Pittsburgh and Carnegie Mellon University are located. Historically, this was Pittsburgh's cultural center, where some of the city's finest museums and libraries are located.

- **Shadyside** is upscale and has boutique shopping on Walnut Street, as well as some fine bistros, bars, and restaurants. Europeans often say that this part of town is most similar to "home" in terms of lifestyle.

- **The Strip District** is where you get the best fresh fish, vegetables, ethnic foods, and cheese. There are excellent early morning markets, as well as a few good restaurants and nightclubs.

- **Squirrel Hill** is a neighborhood next to Oakland where many faculty and employees of the surrounding universities live. This area has one of the most stable Jewish populations in the United States. There is a large recent Eastern European immigrant population that also gives this area a distinct flair.

- **Brookline**, **Dormont**, and **Crafton** are three residential communities that provided homes for many decades to the city's steelworkers and other tradespeople. These neighborhoods, as well as others such as the **South Side**, the **North Side**, **Beechview**, and **Overbrook**, have been revitalized in the past several years by young professional homeowners seeking to restore period homes. **East Washington** and **Canonsburg** to the south of Pittsburgh have also experienced their own recent periods of rebirth.

- Traditionally, a list of Pittsburgh's most prestigious addresses would include **Fox Chapel**, **Sewickley**, **Upper St. Clair**, and **Mt. Lebanon**. These neighborhoods have among the best school systems in the country, especially Mount Lebanon, which is a consistent award winner in this area.

- Two of the fastest growing areas near Pittsburgh are **Wexford** and **Cranberry Township**, about 30 minutes north of the city.

Work Ethic

Pittsburghers work hard, as do most Americans. Contrary to myths about the easy life in America, people put in long hours at their jobs. In fact, many American workers enjoy about two weeks of vacation per year, fewer than workers in many industrialized countries. Nationalized economic safety nets such as social security, unemployment benefits, and health care are less extensive than those in some other industrialized countries.

Pittsburgh has much to offer its residents. The region provides diverse high quality work, living conditions, recreation, entertainment, and learning opportunities. The universities, colleges, museums, arts groups, and sports teams are internationally known. It is important to explore the city and region, participate in its activities, and be open to new experiences to appreciate them fully.

History

Located in what is now called the Mid-Atlantic region of the United States, the region where Pittsburgh exists was once the home of tribes of North America's first human occupants, the people we call Native Americans, also known as American Indians. Tribes such as the Delaware, Seneca, Fox, Wyandott, and Shawnee once hunted, farmed, fished, worshipped, and built villages in this area until their civilization largely died out in the 18th and 19th centuries under the pressures of the newly arrived and quickly expanding European settlement.

Pittsburgh was established, grew, and prospered for several key reasons. Its geographical location where the Allegheny, Monongahela, and Ohio Rivers meet provided easy and inexpensive transportation for people and goods all the way to the Mississippi River. The region is still rich in coal and was extremely rich in natural resources including timber. During the 18th century both the French and

British saw the confluence of the three rivers, "the point," as a strategically important location from which to control access to the interior of North America. The French built Fort Duquesne there; its remains can be seen today in Point State Park in the downtown area. When the British defeated the French in The French and Indian War in 1758, the British replaced Fort Duquesne with Fort Pitt.

Pittsburgh's growth into an important American city is directly linked to industry. It was a center of glass, oil, and especially iron and steel production. As the United States developed and the population swelled in the 19th and 20th centuries, Pittsburgh factories and workers produced a large percentage of the steel and machinery needed to build the nation's infrastructure: ports, railways, roads, and cities. During the American Civil War and World Wars I and II, Pittsburgh factories produced the metal and weapons necessary for the wars.

As industry in Pittsburgh grew, a few men became fabulously rich. You will notice that many of the city's largest cultural institutions and landmarks carry the names of industrial and business leaders: Carnegie, Frick, Schenley, Phipps, Mellon, Heinz, and Westinghouse. Factory workers, however, many of them newly arrived immigrants from Eastern Europe, worked and lived in relatively modest conditions. It was not until the growth of the labor union movement in the late 19th and early 20th centuries that work environments, pay, and overall living conditions of city residents began to improve.

Although heavy industry had given Pittsburgh residents a host of problems, it also left the city with the universities, libraries, museums, arts programs, parks, and neighborhoods that are its strengths today. The best way to appreciate how much Pittsburgh has changed is to compare early 20th century photographs of downtown that hang in the Carnegie Library in Oakland with modern photographs of this area taken from Mt. Washington.

Economy

American cities are the product of economic growth and change. We have discussed the innovative vitality of Pittsburgh's new industries. This city, more than any other in the country, displays the topographical effects of construction, destruction, and revitalization. It is also more like the economies of other large American cities. In the past, large steel and machinery manufacturing companies dominated the region's business activity. Today, city and municipal governments welcome small businesses, retail stores, and entertainment businesses such as bars and restaurants.

Some area residents are still recovering from the decline of manufacturing in the last few decades. In spite of this, many give credit for the city's economic revitalization to the growth of high technology, health care, industrial research and development, and financial and educational services. Both the University of Pittsburgh and Carnegie Mellon University have formed partnerships with the private sector to establish new businesses. Of course, manufacturing and big business have not completely disappeared. Pittsburgh continues to have important manufacturing businesses.

Adapting

As a newcomer to the United States and to Pittsburgh, you will likely experience culture shock. Shortly after beginning your stay here, you might begin to have unusual feelings of frustration, homesickness, and extreme shyness. You might feel useless, unable to meet other people, and unable to carry out your daily tasks. You might not know why you feel this way. These feelings are due to the fact that you are in a new and strange country.

Culture shock is a natural reaction to new surroundings and a new culture. Even experienced travelers must deal with culture shock to some extent. The best way to deal with culture shock is to know what it is, understand how it can affect you, and take realistic steps to manage it.

Culture

In order to understand culture shock, it is necessary to understand some things about culture. It is made up of learned behaviors. Culture is everything we say, think, believe, and do. It has two levels: a surface level and a hidden level. Think of the surface level as those aspects of culture

Surface Level	Hidden Level
Manners	Beliefs
Customs	Ideals
Social institutions	Ideas
Ceremonies	Values
Written laws	Unwritten laws
Religion	Morals
Language	Unspoken assumptions
Food	

that you can see immediately: language, religion, and customs. The hidden level contains aspects that are harder to see: ideals, unwritten laws, and values.

Culture Shock

Culture shock is a human reaction to a new culture. It can affect your emotions as well as your body. Emotional effects range from mild unhappiness to severe depression, more rarely, to feelings of panic. Effects on your body include stress, loss of appetite, or even an increased appetite.

We know that culture shock causes different reactions in different people. Your experience with it will be different from what others experience; it is not predictable. It does not happen suddenly, nor does it have a single way of affecting you. It can build up slowly and change your thoughts, feelings, and behavior. You might experience culture shock early in your stay or after months of living and working here. It is possible that you will experience periods of highs and lows over the course of many months.

Culture shock happens because you have left familiar surroundings. Most noticeably, everything that was easy and automatic for you at home has become difficult. At home, you knew how to greet neighbors, how to take the bus, and where to shop. In Pittsburgh, perhaps you never see your neighbors, there is no bus near your home, and you do not know where to shop. You discover that you have to relearn the most basic rules of living in a community.

Culture shock also happens for several other reasons:

- **Lack of information.** You do not know how to act in everyday situations. Everyday and world events happen without your knowing about them. You feel cut off from the world.

- **Unrealistic goals.** Your high hopes about what you would do, learn, and accomplish are not coming true as quickly as you had hoped.

- **Inability to see results.** You are making a great effort to learn your new language, to progress on projects at work, and to meet new people, but you have nothing to show for your efforts.

- **Expectations.** Many things you thought were true about your new country are not true.

- **Change of environment.** Your surroundings are strange. Everything here seems difficult and takes much longer.

- **Ambiguity.** It is difficult to find clear, understandable answers to your questions.

You might feel ready to accept your new surroundings one day, but feel depressed, angry, and homesick the next. The sidebar on the next page lists common culture shock symptoms.

Managing Culture Shock

There are ways to manage culture shock to ease your adjustment to life in the United States. Making a successful adjustment involves some skill and knowledge, work, patience, and persistence. You can cultivate a positive, realistic attitude toward adjustment if you:

- **Have a sense of humor.** Maintain your sense of humor so that you will be better able to keep both successes and failures in perspective. A sense of humor will help you prevent failures from getting you down, making you feel unhappy, ineffective, and discouraged.

- **Set realistic goals and be task oriented.** Cultural adjustment is a slow process that can take months, even years. At times you might see so much to do and learn that you feel overwhelmed. Instead of rushing and feeling pressured to adjust quickly, expect to make slow, steady progress. In fact, your goal should be to progress, not necessarily to arrive at a point where you are completely adjusted to life in the United States. Set realistic, attainable goals. Divide large and difficult projects into smaller tasks that you can finish one by one.

Symptoms of culture shock

- Homesickness: persistent feelings of sadness about being far from home.
- Withdrawal: avoiding the host culture by spending excessive amounts of time reading, or spending time only with fellow nationals.
- Marital stress: marriage problems can sometimes be a result of the stress of moving to a new environment.
- Family tension and conflict
- Boredom
- Excessive sleeping
- Stereotyping host nationals
- Hostility toward host nationals
- Depression

Have a tolerance for failure. Large and small failures during cultural adjustment are inevitable and normal. When you fail, think about what you can learn from your failure and how you will recover. In the end, failure itself is not serious. Not recovering because you are discouraged, however, can be disastrous.

As you adjust, learn, and progress in your new surroundings, keep this advice in mind:

- **Look for reasons that explain behavior around you.** Ask why people act the way they do rather than explain away their behavior as illogical. Try looking at events from an American's point of view. You will not always be able to find good explanations, but the effort of searching for reasons will prevent you from making quick and unfair judgments. Also, talk to people from your home country who have lived in the area. Ask them for information.

- **Relax your grip on your culture.** Try to adopt some aspects of American culture rather than resist them. Too much resistance can frustrate and discourage you. Of course, this is not a suggestion that you abandon your culture.

- **Contact a host national or an organization such as the Pittsburgh Council for International Visitors to be your cultural informant.** After spending some time in the United States, you will meet people and begin to make friendships. A trusted friend might be able to explain American manners, attitudes, and behavior. Keep in mind that opinions vary widely. Some people are more observant than others.

Understanding Where You Come From

One of the most important pieces of knowledge you will acquire as you adjust to life in the United States is a better understanding of your own culture and how it has made you develop as a person. Although you might understand your home country well, the experience of living in another culture offers a new and unique opportunity to consider yourself and your home.

American Culture

What is American culture?

Because the United States is so prominent in the world, it is the subject of many myths, misinformed opinions, and wrong predictions. There are some classic myths about the country and its people that cover a wide range of views. Some believe the United States is a wealthy country where immigrants get rich quick without working hard. Others think of the United States as a crime ridden nation run by heartless businessmen.

You probably already have some ideas, opinions, and fears about American people. There is no way to predict whether or not your ideas will prove to be true or false. The most important advice to keep in mind as you adjust to living in the United States is not to let your expectations determine how you deal with Americans.

American Cultural Characteristics

Time

Americans keep appointment calendars and live according to schedules. They always seem to be in a hurry, and this might make them seem abrupt in manner.

Americans are generally more concerned with the present. They want to know about the condition of things as they are now. Additionally, Americans like to think of the near future. They believe that one can accurately make plans for three to five years into the future.

Americans consider themselves doers. That is, they place great value on those people who take individual initiative, show self-confidence, and achieve results.

Communication

Americans place importance on verbal communication. They show respect by making eye contact, responding to, and interacting actively with a speaker. Active listening and speaking are signs that a dialogue is taking place.

American communication patterns are direct. Two American proverbs best demonstrate this idea: "Say what you mean; mean what you say," and "Honesty is the best policy."

Americans tend not to be overly emotional when speaking. This is more true for the workplace or business environment than for a social situation.

When calling a person, even a friend, during his or her working hours, Americans often do not encourage much small talk; they ask their questions or give the needed information and then end the call. This is not meant to be rude or unfriendly; both of you might be busy and this is a business call, not a social call.

Communication can be informal as well. Americans like to dress informally, entertain informally, and treat each other informally, even when there is a great difference in age or in social standing. They often call each other by their first names, rather than use Mr. or Ms. followed by a last name. Students and professors often call each other by their first names. Using someone's first name is not considered rude. When you are unsure about whether or not it is appropriate to call someone by their first name, simply ask. Asking "Would you prefer I call you by your first name or use your last name?" is a considerate way to find out.

It is not unusual for Americans to give many compliments. To some other cultures, this might seem insincere. The usual and expected response is "Thank you."

American culture is verbal. Misunderstandings can occur if one person tries to communicate non-verbally and the other does not understand or misinterprets the message. For example, in restaurants it is rude to snap your fingers to call someone over. Generally, a person will say, "Excuse me," to catch a waiter's attention.

To avoid misunderstandings, Americans often use verbal feedback when listening. Some common expressions that show someone is listening are "I see," "Mm-hmm," "Oh, sure," "Okay," and "I understand." In American culture, it is usually acceptable to interrupt another speaker so that you can make sure you understand what the speaker said.

Understanding

When communicating, it is the duty of the listener to make sure that he or she understands completely. Communication moves both ways. Here are some active listening and speaking rules:

- You have the right to understand. Let a speaker know when you do not understand.

- Check to make sure that what you understood is correct.

- Insist on your right to understand. You can politely interrupt a conversation when you have stopped understanding. Stopping others in the middle of conversations is normal and expected in order to make your understanding clear. Here are some polite phrases you can use:

"Excuse me, I did not understand what you said."
"Can you repeat that?"
"What does that mean?"
"I do not understand."
"Can you explain it to me another way?"
"Do you understand what I am saying?"
"Am I explaining myself clearly?"
"Did I answer your question?"

You can also repeat facts such as times, dates, names as a question to confirm if they are correct or not. You can also repeat essential information. For example, "Let me make sure I understand. You said that . . . "

When invited to a dinner or party, Americans generally say, "Yes, I can come." or "I am sorry, but I will not be able to make it." If a person accepts an invitation, Americans expect a guest to arrive. If it is not possible to attend, it is preferable to say this directly. It is not rude to decline an invitation. It is considered rude, even untruthful, to accept an invitation when you know you will not be able to attend.

When an American corrects someone, he or she usually begins with a word or expression to soften disagreement. For example, a phrase such as "Uhm," "Well," "I think" or "Actually," can be used before disagreeing.

Americans smile a lot. This is meant to show friendliness.

Space

Americans value privacy and like their space. American houses and offices are often big and open.

On an interpersonal level, Americans tend to maintain a three-foot-diameter "space bubble" between people. Introductions are often accompanied by a firm but brief handshake. When Americans talk to each other, they tend to stand about an arm's length apart. You might notice that Americans say, "Excuse me," for even the slightest accidental touching of another person.

Power

Americans value equality. Although not inclined toward strict hierarchical orders, they do respect authority figures. This respect is earned by showing respect to and appreciation of subordinates.

Americans are generally not class conscious. They do not consider themselves superior or inferior to others based on class or family. More respect might be shown toward those who are older or perceived as having more status.

Individualism

Americans are individualistic. First and foremost, they view themselves as individuals. From childhood, children are taught to be independent. In contrast to most other cultures, Americans choose their own schools, select their own course of study in college, plan their own careers, and arrange their own marriages instead of following a parental plan.

Americans also prefer laws, policies, and rules that are applied equally to all.

Competitiveness

Americans are competitive yet cooperative. They place a high value on achievement, and this leads them to compete with each other.

You will find friendly and not-so-friendly competition everywhere. The American style of friendly joking or banter, of getting the last word in, and the quick and witty reply are subtle forms of competition.

Although often competitive, Americans also have a good sense of teamwork—cooperating with others to achieve a goal.

Structure

Americans are flexible. They have less fear of uncertainty than do most other cultures. The general mindset of the American is to constantly find new and better ways of doing something.

Thinking

Americans are inductive and linear. That is, they will be persuaded in an argument only if there is quantitative data to support this argument. American thought is founded on concrete proof, not on theories or ideas.

Socializing with Americans

During your stay in Pittsburgh, you will probably be invited to have dinner with an American family in their home. The following information and rules will help you to feel more comfortable about your visit.

- **When Meals are Served.** Most Americans eat lunch at approximately 12:00 noon. The evening meal, or dinner, may be served as early as 6:00 PM (especially if the hosts have young children) or as late as 8:00 PM. Most Americans do not serve dinner later than 8:00 PM. Brunch (a combination of breakfast and lunch) is usually served in the late morning or at 12:00 noon.

- **Gifts.** Americans do not expect gifts when they invite people to their homes. If you wish to bring a gift, it is appropriate to bring the hostess flowers or candy. If you are attending a dinner party, you may wish to bring a bottle of wine.

- **When to Arrive.** Your hosts will expect you to arrive at the time that they suggest that you arrive. For example, if your host asks you to arrive at 6:00

PM, it would be considered impolite if you arrive at 7:00 PM. If you must be late, always call your hosts to inform them that you will be late.

- **What to wear.** At informal dinners, most men wear casual slacks and a shirt or sweater. Women usually wear casual dresses or pants outfits. If you have questions as to what you should wear to a dinner or luncheon, always call your hosts and ask them. In the summer, most dinners (especially "barbecues") are very informal.

- **RSVP.** If you are sent a formal invitation to an event, you will probably be asked to RSVP by a certain date. This means that you should call the host to accept or decline the invitation by that date. It is considered impolite if you do not call the host when you are asked to RSVP.

- **"Pot Luck" Dinners.** You may be invited to a "pot luck" dinner party. That means that each guest is expected to bring some type of food to share with the other guests. Most hosts will ask that you bring a specific type of food, such as a salad or dessert.

Your hosts will always want you to feel at ease in their home. If you have any food allergies or allergies to dogs or cats, call your hosts about your concerns in advance of your dinner.

American Holidays

All Americans celebrate several holidays throughout the year. Schools, federal buildings, post offices, and banks close for the day on national holidays such as New Year's Day and Independence Day. Other holidays are informal or religious. Depending on your faith, you might or might not celebrate them. Here are some of the best known, widely celebrated holidays.

New Year's Day, January 1
Schools, business offices, the post office, and other federal offices are closed. Most people actually celebrate the new year the night before. Traditionally, people attend parties and count down the last ten seconds before midnight and the official start of a new year. Pittsburgh has a "First Night" celebration on New Year's Eve in the center of the city. This is a non-alcoholic family event with fireworks and entertainment.

Martin Luther King Day, Third Monday in January
Federal offices and post offices close. Some schools and business offices close. This is a new national holiday to commemorate Dr. Martin Luther King, Jr., the famous civil rights leader. Many community groups organize special presentations about Dr. King and civil rights in the United States on this day.

Groundhog Day, February 2
An American folk holiday celebrating the coming of spring. According to folk belief, if a groundhog leaves its hole where it sleeps during the winter and sees its shadow, there will be six more weeks of winter weather. If it does not, spring will soon arrive. The most famous celebration of this day is held in Punxatawny, Pennsylvania, a small town located two hours away from Pittsburgh.

Valentine's Day, February 14
An informal, nonreligious holiday when lovers, husbands, wives, boyfriends, and girlfriends exchange small gifts such as flowers, cards, or candy as a sign of affection.

St. Patrick's Day, March 17
The tradition of celebrating St. Patrick's day in the United States was brought by Irish immigrants. Now, St. Patrick's Day is a day to celebrate all things Irish. There are parades, people dress in green clothes, go to parties, and drink Irish and green colored beer. Pittsburgh has one of the largest St. Patrick's Day parades in the country due in part to its large Irish population.

Passover, between late March and early April
A Jewish holiday also recognized in Christian church services. Passover celebrates the Israelites' deliverance from bondage in Egypt three thousand years ago.

Good Friday and **Easter**, in March, April or early May
A Christian holiday. Good Friday commemorates the day Christians believe Jesus was crucified. Easter, three days later on a Sunday, commemorates the day he rose from the dead. On Good Friday, most business offices, post offices, and federal offices stay open, although they might close earlier than usual. Some schools close.

Mother's Day, second Sunday in May
A day to honor mothers. Sons and daughters give their mothers small gifts, make dinner for them, or take them to a restaurant.

Memorial Day, last Monday in May
Schools, business offices, the post office, and federal offices are closed. Memorial Day honors those who fought and died in wars.

Father's Day, second Sunday in June
A day to honor fathers. Sons and daughters give their fathers small gifts as signs of affection and appreciation.

Independence Day, July 4
Schools, business offices, the post office, and federal offices are closed. This day commemorates the day the British colonies declared independence from England and formed the United States of America in 1776. Today, Americans celebrate Independence Day with fireworks and picnics or cookouts with friends and family in parks and backyards. The best fireworks display in Pittsburgh is downtown at the Point.

Labor Day, first Monday in September
Schools, business offices, the post office, and federal offices are closed. This day commemorates workers of all trades. Pittsburgh has one of the largest Labor Day parades in the country.

Rosh Hashanah and **Yom Kippur**, between mid-September and mid-October
Rosh Hashanah is the "New Year" according to the Jewish calendar. Yom Kippur, ten days later, is known as a "Day of Atonement" when Jews ask for forgiveness and reconciliation.

Halloween, October 31
Although this holiday is also celebrated in other countries and has roots in old religious rituals, it has become a children's holiday in the United States. On Halloween, children dress up in costumes and go door to door in their neighborhoods asking for candy, which is called "trick or treating." Some communities have parades for children, and adults often have costume parties.

   If your children go trick or treating, be sure to inspect the candy they bring home to see if it is safe to eat. It is a good idea to talk to a neighbor about how people on your street organize Halloween night.

Thanksgiving, fourth Thursday in November
Schools, business offices, the post office, and federal offices are closed. It is a widely celebrated nonreligious, family holiday that commemorates the first European settlers in the United States. On Thanksgiving Day, American families gather to have a large dinner, and turkey is traditionally served. Pittsburgh has an annual Thanksgiving Day Parade the Saturday following Thanksgiving.

Hanukkah, in November or December
Jewish holiday that lasts for eight days. This holiday, the "Festival of Lights," commemorates the rededication of the great Temple in Jerusalem. Today, Jews celebrate Hanukkah by singing and praying, giving gifts to children, and playing special games.

Christmas, December 25
A Christian holiday widely celebrated in the United States. The day commemorates the birth of Jesus. In the United States, Christians attend special Christmas services, spend the day with family, and exchange presents. Many families set up and decorate a Christmas tree in their houses. Some Eastern Orthodox Christians celebrate the same holiday in early January. Christmas has become so large and commercialized that is has become an entire *season* known as the Christmas or holiday season. Stores in downtown Pittsburgh are decorated with lights and there are many holiday events for families scheduled in the city during this time.

Kwaanza, December
Some Americans of African descent also celebrate Kwaanza, an eight-day festival that celebrates traditional African values, including unity, family, and responsibility. Although Kwaanza is not celebrated with gift giving, it does involve a variety of community events.

Volunteers

Thousands of Americans of all ages volunteer for non-profit organizations each year. A volunteer is a person who donates his or her services. Men, women, and teenagers volunteer at hospitals, museums, schools, service organizations, religious organizations, youth programs, or other programs that enrich the lives of people in their communities. Volunteerism is a way of life in America. Many non-profit organizations such as the Pittsburgh Council for International Visitors rely on volunteers to carry out their programs.

Americans choose to volunteer for organizations for many reasons. You may choose to become a volunteer to meet people, to improve your English or your professional skills, to learn about your community or to help others. All volunteers share the feeling that they can make a difference in their community by helping others.

Volunteering may be very satisfying to you. To become a volunteer, choose an organization that interests you or would benefit from your special skills. For example, if you love animals, you may choose to volunteer at the Pittsburgh Zoo. Volunteers may answer telephones, enter data in a computer, interact with people, or give tours, among many other types of duties. Each non-profit organization will have different types of tasks for volunteers.

If you are interested in becoming a volunteer, you may wish to ask your American contacts for suggestions, call an organization listed in the Yellow Pages under "Social Service Organizations" and ask to speak with their volunteer coordinator, or call the United Way's Volunteer Referral Line for their Good Neighbors program at (412) 261-6010. You may choose to volunteer on a weekly basis or volunteer for special projects through volunteer organizations such as Pittsburgh Cares [(412) 471-2114].

Organizations to Help You Adapt

There are several organizations that will assist you or members of your family in adapting to Pittsburgh. PCIV offers programming for individuals and families, including dinners with host families, volunteer opportunities for spouses, and the arrangement of professional meetings, tours, and seminars. The three women's groups offer informational, entertaining, and participatory programming for international spouses.

The telephone numbers for the women's organizations on the right are home numbers of members of these groups.

Pittsburgh Council for International Visitors (PCIV)   412-624-7800

International Women's Association of Pittsburgh
(Oakland Area)   412-441-8102 or
                       412-683-1691

International Women's Group
(North Hills area)   412-486-0774 or
                           412-486-5334

International Women's Club
(Monroeville area)   724-733-1001

L a w

Your Legal Status

There are two main types of visa status for foreigners living in the United States: Immigrant and Non-Immigrant visa status. Whether or not you can work here and how many times you can leave the United States and return is determined by your visa. Visas are issued and regulated by the **Immigration and Naturalization Service** (INS). Their Pittsburgh office is downtown in the Federal Building at 1000 Liberty Avenue, 3rd Floor. You can get information and talk to an INS representative at 1-800-688-9889.

Immigrant Visas

If you are a legal immigrant in the United States, you will have either a "green card" (newer cards are pink and are called "pink cards") or a "white card." Regular legal immigrants have green cards that allow them to work. They can leave and return to the United States as often and as many times as they wish. White cards are issued to immigrants who have refugee status. They are allowed the same work and travel benefits. If you have one of these cards, and have lived in the United States for five years, you can apply to become a U.S. citizen. Contact the INS at the address above for more information.

Non-Immigrant Visas

There are several types of non-immigrant visas. Each type is designated by a letter. Two common types for foreigners living in the Pittsburgh area are *F* visas for students and *L* visas for employees transferred to the United States by a company.

Your work status is determined by your visa. In many cases, students who have an *F* visa can work a limited number of hours per week in order to earn some extra money to pay for school expenses. Company employees who have *L* visas are authorized to work. However, an employee's spouse and children, who might also hold a special *L* visa, are often not authorized to work.

It is important that you understand your visa status to avoid problems when you travel outside the United States or change your plans. If you decide to stay in the United States longer than you originally planned, graduate from school, or get married or divorced, you must change your visa status. Call the INS at the phone number above to find out which forms and documents you need to complete.

Gathering documents, making telephone calls, and fulfilling INS document processing requirements take a lot of time. As a rule, you should start preparing your application for visa changes as early as possible.

If you are having exceptional problems, you can talk to a lawyer who specializes in immigration law. **The American Immigration Lawyers Association** in Washington, D.C., can refer you to a lawyer experienced in immigration law in Pittsburgh who might be able to advise you. Their telephone number is 202-371-9377.

Resident Status

Whatever your visa status, if you are living in the Pittsburgh area, you are a resident of either the city or the suburb where you live. You are also a resident of Allegheny County, or a surrounding county, and the State of Pennsylvania. As a resident, you benefit from some public services, such as the right for your children to attend public schools in your district. If you work, you will have to pay local, state, and federal taxes. Unless you are a U.S. citizen, however, you cannot vote or hold public office. Anyone in the United States, whether a resident or nonresident, must follow all U.S. laws.

Identification

As you settle in to life in the area, you will begin to search for a place to live, arrange utilities for your home, and enroll your children in a school. At various times in the process, you and your family members will be asked to provide some form of identification.

Different organizations will ask for different kinds of identification. Your passport is your primary official identification document. You might also be asked to provide a birth certificate, an official document that states your name, parents' names, place of birth, and the year you were born. Because all Americans have a birth certificate, some of the organizations you contact might assume you have one too. If you do not have your country's version of a birth certificate, contact officials in your country and try to get one. If this is impossible, simply explaining why you do not have one might satisfy an organization. They might ask you to supply an alternative document in its place.

You should not carry your passport with you every day. It is difficult to replace a lost passport. You should make photocopies of your passport and visas and keep both at home in a safe place. Only carry your passport when you need it as an original document.

Most Americans use their driver's license as their primary, everyday identification card. If you do not have one, you can apply for a Pennsylvania non-driver identification card at the **Department of Transportation** in the Pennsylvania State Office Building downtown at 300 Liberty Avenue, Wednesday through Friday, 8:30 a.m. to 3:30 p.m.

Social Security Number

When you begin to arrange services such as obtaining electricity service for your home, opening a bank account, and applying for credit cards, you might be asked for a Social Security number. These numbers are assigned by the Social Security Administration and are often used as identification numbers when paying taxes and applying for government services.

Until recently, foreign residents and their family members could get Social Security numbers. However, new laws restrict who can and cannot get a number. The process has become more complicated and whether or not you can get a number depends on your needs. You can call the **Social Security Administration** to ask if you qualify for a number at 1-800-772-1213. If your case is unusual, you can make an appointment to speak with a Social Security representative. The Social Security office in Pittsburgh is located downtown at 915 Penn Avenue.

If you work and pay taxes, you can apply for a Social Security number. You can also apply for numbers for your dependents—family members who depend on you for support such as your children. However, your spouse (husband or wife) is not considered your dependent.

You do *not* need a Social Security number in order to arrange some services including:

- purchasing savings bonds
- opening a bank account or conducting business at a financial institution
- registering for school
- applying for school lunch programs

In some cases, you will need a Social Security number to receive government services. You might be asked for a Social Security number for these services. Even if you do not work, you might be able to apply for a number. When you contact the Social Security office in Pittsburgh, you will need to give them certain documents

Pittsburgh Area Consuls

Austria
Mr. Edgar Braun
ARUS Andritz-Ruthner
Southpointe
  Industrial Park
125 Technology Drive
Canonsburg, PA 15317
Tel: 724-745-7599
Fax: 724-745-9570

Belgium
Mrs. Ann Lackner
700 Bell Avenue
Carnegie Office Park
Pittsburgh, PA 15106
Tel: 412-279-2121
Fax: 412-279-6426

Denmark
Mr. George Knapp
Royal Danish Consulate
201 South Craig Street
Pittsburgh, PA 15213
Tel: 412-782-7253
Fax: 412-782-7231

France
Mr. J. P. Collet
Pittsburgh Corning Corp.
800 Presque Isle Drive
Pittsburgh, PA 15239
Tel: 724-327-2911
Fax: 724-733-4815

Germany
Mr. Michael E. Gerlach
Mannesmann Demag Corp.
345 Rouser Road
Airport Office Park, Bldg. 5
Coraopolis, PA 15108
Tel: 412-604-0135
Fax: 412-269-5478

Guatemala
Mrs. Margarita Winikoff
709 Washington Drive
Pittsburgh, PA 15229
Tel: 412-366-7715

Italy
Mr. Joseph D'Andrea
419 Wood Street
Pittsburgh, PA 15222
Tel: 412-391-7669
Fax: 412-391-9936

Malta
Dr. Anthony Debons
115 Edgecliff Road
Carnegie, PA 15106
Tel: 412-279-6170

Slovak Republic
Mr. Joseph T. Senko
Arbor Professional Centre,
Suite 203
275 Curry Hollow Road
Pittsburgh, PA 15236
Tel: 412-653-9200
Fax: 412-653-9206

Switzerland
Dr. Heinz W. Kunz
PO Box 7379
Pittsburgh, PA 15213
Tel: 412-621-8804
Fax: 412-621-9611

United Kingdom
Mr. William R. Newlin
Buchanan Ingersoll Prof.
Corp.
One Oxford Center
301 Grant Street
Pittsburgh, PA 15219
Tel: 412-562-8872
Fax: 412-391-0910

Consulates in New York City

Canada
212-596-1700 or
716-852-1252

Mexico
212-689-0460

India
212-879-7809 or
212-879-7806

Russia
212-348-0926

UK
212-745-0200

Japan
212-371-8222

China
212-330-7409

including your visa, passport, and a letter from the government agency providing
the service that states that you:

- need a Social Security number
- qualify to receive their services
- are the applicant
- are required by law to have a Social Security number

Consulates

Many nations do not maintain a consulate in the Pittsburgh area. If you do not see
a consul from your country in the list opposite, you will have to contact the
consulate in New York City. You can get the telephone numbers of your consulate
in New York or Washington, D.C., by calling the **U.S. State Department, Bureau
of Consular Affairs** at 202-647-1488 or on the Internet from the State Department
at http://travel.state.gov.

Behavior Laws: Smoking, Drinking Alcohol, Sexual Harassment and Theft

As a newcomer to the United States, you should be aware of laws concerning
smoking, drinking alcohol, and sexual harassment.

To best understand these laws, keep in mind two observations. First, they reflect
American culture and attempts to stop or limit behavior seen as harmful to
individuals and society. Second, these laws are enforced both officially and
informally. If you violate them, you risk paying fines, or, more rarely, spending time
in prison. Those who break these laws are sometimes seen by friends and colleagues
as rude and unprofessional.

Cigarettes and Smoking

Much of American society's acceptance of smoking, especially in public spaces, has
decreased rapidly over the past few years. Although smoking is still socially
acceptable, smoking in certain places is not legally permitted. Anti-smoking laws
have been primarily motivated by public health concerns.

Smoking in any public space, publicly or privately owned, is generally
prohibited. Public space includes airplanes, public transportation, office buildings,
hallways, and lobbies. You will notice that office workers stand outside office
buildings, even in cold weather to take smoking breaks. You can still smoke in

homes, bars, clubs, and smoking sections of restaurants. It is considered polite and considerate to ask non-smokers for permission before lighting a cigarette in their presence.

A person under 18 years of age cannot buy cigarettes. Do not be surprised or offended if a cashier asks to see proof of age (identification) such as your driver's license. They are required by law to check the age of anyone who looks young (under 27 years of age) and wants to buy cigarettes.

Buying and Drinking Alcohol

Drinking alcohol is generally acceptable in American society. As in many cultures, it is prominent in social settings and during certain special occasions. In American society, however, opinions about the acceptability of drinking range from those who would prohibit alcohol to those who believe that drinking is simply a personal choice.

Adult Americans often drink during special occasions, both formal and informal, such as special dinners, holidays, parties, and receptions. Drinking a beer in a bar after work or during the weekend, especially when watching sports, is common. However, adults rarely drink wine or beer during everyday lunches and dinners. Parents especially tend to limit drinking when children are present for fear of setting a bad example.

The most important law to know is that anyone under 21 cannot buy or drink alcohol in Pennsylvania. Bars and clubs that serve alcohol often prohibit anyone under 21 from entering. Club and bar employees might ask to see proof of age before allowing you to enter or serving you alcohol. Occasionally, in a family setting in a private home, adults under 21 may drink alcohol. (See page 61 for information about the consequences of drinking and driving.)

Sexual Harassment

Tolerance of sexual harassment in the United States and many other countries is decreasing rapidly. In the United States, where both the law and unwritten social rules powerfully affect social behavior, all forms of harassment are unacceptable. Newcomers should be aware that those who sexually harass others suffer serious, negative consequences. Lawsuits related to sexual harassment in the workplace can and do happen. More commonly, however, friendships as well as personal and professional reputations can be quickly ruined.

Defining sexual harassment is sometimes difficult. Based on your own culture and experiences, you might or might not know what is appropriate in the United

States. In any case, U.S. laws apply to all persons. Some acts are clearly cases of unacceptable sexual harassment. Written messages, spoken suggestions, jokes, and touching that intentionally or unintentionally degrades or intimidate others is unacceptable. Other cases are less clear and depend more on personalities and setting. Generally speaking, touching a co-worker anywhere except the arm or shoulder might be considered harassment. It is often acceptable to show interest in another person by asking him or her to go out on a date. In some cases, however, asking out a co-worker might be inappropriate at work although it might be appropriate to ask out the same person when in a social place, such as a bar.

Misunderstandings do happen. For example, someone can perceive an innocent joke or comment, which was intended only to be funny, as harassment.

Shoplifting

Most stores in the United States use hidden security cameras to watch customers as they shop. When you are inside a store to do your shopping, always keep store items fully visible until you have paid for them. Do not put an item inside your purse or in your pocket until you have paid for it, or you could be accused of theft, arrested, and pay a heavy fine. The incident could also be made a part of your permanent record.

Personal Safety

Cities in the United States have a bad reputation for crime. But crime levels in most American cities have decreased significantly over the past few years.

As does any large American city, Pittsburgh has problems with crime. Yet, the number of crimes in Pittsburgh has always been relatively low. Some common kinds of crime are: car theft, burglary, mugging, and rape. You might also hear about shootings. Unlikely many countries, it is easy to buy and own a gun in the United States. Most people, however, do not own guns.

Here is some practical safety advice for your stay in Pittsburgh:

At Home

Always lock all windows and doors when you leave home.

Install or have your landlord install strong deadbolt locks, which you can buy at a hardware store.

Light the outside of your front and back doors at night. Thieves hate lights. Use a timer to turn interior lights on and off when you are not home to make your house look occupied. Hardware stores sell motion detection lights that turn on when someone walks by.

Do not allow strangers, including repairpeople, into your house unless you called them first. Ask for company identification even if you did call for a repairperson. Meter readers from your natural gas company often wear identification on the outside of their uniforms.

Do not put your address on your key chain.

The **Pittsburgh Police** offer a free burglary prevention service. A police officer will come to your house or apartment and tell you how to make it safer. Call **412-244-4180**. If you live outside the city, call your local police department and ask if they offer a similar service.

Walking Around

Do not carry large amounts of cash. Use a credit card or checks to make large purchases.

Do not wear excessive amounts of jewelry—especially gold chains.

Do not count large amounts of money where others can see you.

Discourage pickpockets. Keep your purse closed. Keep your wallet in a safe place such as your front pocket.

Do not go out alone at night—walk with other people.

Be cautious when walking outside at night. Be alert. Stay where there are a lot of people.

Avoid dark alleys and streets. Walk in well-lit areas.

If you are lost, do not look lost because you might look like an easy target. Always walk with purpose as if you know where you are going.

If you are being followed by someone on foot, cross the street or change direction. Go into a store and call the police.

If you are held-up, do not resist. Give up your wallet quickly and quietly.

Carry a whistle that makes a loud, high pitched sound.

Car

Always lock your car doors.

Park in well-lit areas.

Do not leave packages or expensive items in plain view. Lock them in the trunk.

If you park in a parking garage and feel unsafe walking to your car at night, ask an attendant for an escort to walk with you to your car.

You may consider buying special locks to prevent expensive stereos from being stolen out of your car.

If you have an expensive car, consider buying a car alarm or a "club" to put on your steering wheel. A "club" is a steel bar that you lock to your steering wheel to deter theft when you are not driving your car. You can buy a club at hardware and automotive stores.

Lock your doors when driving at night.

Do not pick up strangers when you drive.

Police

If you are the victim of any crime in the City of Pittsburgh, call the Pittsburgh Police at **911**. This telephone number is different from conventional phone numbers—it is shorter, easier to remember, and faster to call.

If you live in a suburb of Pittsburgh, you must call a different phone number to contact the police. Each suburb has its own police force and its own phone numbers to call for an ambulance or the fire department. You can find emergency numbers in the first section of both the White and Yellow Pages telephone books.

When you call the police, listen to the police operator and follow any instructions that he or she gives you over the phone. Try to remain calm and speak slowly when you contact the police. If you call away from home, you will need to be able to tell them where you are. Look for street signs.

If someone breaks into your house or apartment, do not touch anything or clean up any damage caused by the thief. The police need to investigate by searching your home, taking fingerprints, and looking for evidence.

If you arrive home and discover that your door is open, do not go inside. Call the police immediately from your neighbor's home or from a public telephone.

Emergency Phone Numbers

As soon as you get a telephone in your home, look up the emergency phone numbers for the police, fire department, ambulance, and poison center in your area, write them down, and keep them next to your phone. Do not wait until an emergency happens to find the numbers in your telephone book!

In the city of Pittsburgh, the emergency phone number to contact the **Pittsburgh Police, Fire Department**, and **Ambulance** is the same: **911**.

Poison Center

If you have a small child, you should also write down the phone number of the **Poison Center: 412-681-6669.**

The poison center will tell you what to do if your child accidentally swallows any household chemical such as soap, cleanser, or medicine.

Other Important Services and Phone Numbers

Pittsburgh Action Against Rape (PAAR) provides counseling services and support to victims of sexual violence. If you are the victim of an attack, they can send a Medical Advocate to meet you at a hospital. Their 24-hour crisis phone number is 412-765-2731.

If you are raped, resist the urge to clean yourself: do not take a shower, brush your hair, or brush your teeth. Even though you might want to wash, the police need to collect evidence to help them find and prosecute the attacker. Go to a hospital and call **Pittsburgh Action Against Rape** at 412-765-2731.

If your spouse has hit you or you feel in danger that your spouse will hurt you, you can get help. **Women's Center and Shelter** offers support and protection to women who are victims of spousal abuse. You can call them at **412-687-8017**. **Women of Hope** also provides support to abused women. Call **412-261-5363**.

Contact Pittsburgh has a 24-hour crisis helpline. You can call Contact Pittsburgh and talk to someone about any emotional problem. All calls are confidential and you can remain anonymous. Trained volunteers can also refer you to social services. They maintain a special phone number for children.

Contact Pittsburgh Helplines

Pittsburgh and North 412-782-4023	**West** 412-787-HELP (4357)
South 412-343-HELP (4357)	**Norwin and McKeesport** 412-864-HELP (4357)
East 412-737-HELP (4357)	**Kidline** 1-800-587-5100

Communications

Mail

Your mail is delivered to your home every day except Sundays and national holidays. Mail carriers leave mail in your mailbox, a special box placed outside your front door or located in the lobby of your apartment building. If you want to mail letters, you can put stamps on them and leave them in your mailbox for the carrier to pick up, take them to a post office, or put them in one of the blue mailboxes located on street corners.

American Addresses

When you send a letter to someone in the United States, write the name, house or apartment number, street name, city or town, state, and ZIP code in the center of the envelope. The ZIP code is a five-digit (sometimes nine-digit) number that you must write as part of a U.S. address. The fifty states are identified by the U.S. post office with two-letter abbreviations. See page 31 for a list of two-letter abbreviations of U.S. state names used by the post office.

You should also put your return address in the upper left corner of the envelope. Your return address enables the post office to return your letter to you if they cannot deliver it.

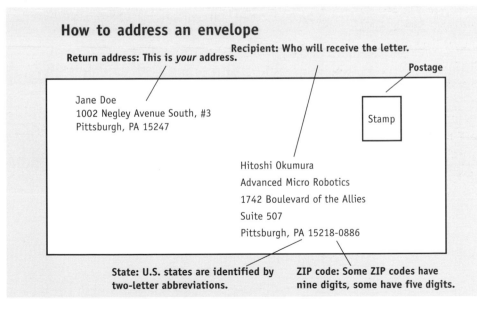

How to address an envelope

Recipient: Who will receive the letter.
Return address: This is *your* address.
Postage

Jane Doe
1002 Negley Avenue South, #3
Pittsburgh, PA 15247

Stamp

Hitoshi Okumura
Advanced Micro Robotics
1742 Boulevard of the Allies
Suite 507
Pittsburgh, PA 15218-0886

State: U.S. states are identified by two-letter abbreviations.

ZIP code: Some ZIP codes have nine digits, some have five digits.

U.S. Postal Service Rates and Times*

Service	Price	Time
Letter anywhere in the U.S.	$.32	2 to 3 days
Postcard anywhere in U.S.	$.20	2 to 3 days
International letter	$.60	depends on destination
International postcard	$.50	depends on destination
U.S. priority mail (2-pound limit)	$3	2 days (or longer)
Express mail	depends on weight	next day
Global (International)	depends on weight	2 to 3 days

*As of May-June 1998. Subject to change.

If you are mailing a letter to another country, do not forget to write the name of the country in English and include "U.S.A." in your return address.

Post Office

The U.S. Post Office has locations in most sections of Pittsburgh and in almost every suburb. The downtown office is on the corner of Grant and Seventh Street. You will find a complete listing by area in the blue section of your White Pages telephone directory.

You can send letters and packages and buy stamps in U.S. post offices. Post offices are generally open Monday through Friday from 8:00 or 8:30 a.m. to 5:00 p.m. and 8:00 or 8:30 a.m. to 12:00 or 1:00 p.m. on Saturdays. They are closed on Sundays and national holidays.

The time it takes for a letter to arrive at an address in another country varies greatly. On average it takes two weeks for a letter to arrive, but the time can vary from one week to two months!

You can also send letters and packages as certified, registered, and insured.

Although you can rent a post office box at the post office, most Americans receive their mail at home. Generally, delivery is on time and dependable.

Receiving and Sending Packages

You can send and receive international packages at the post office. If someone in another country sends you a package, it will be delivered to your home. However, if you have to pay a customs charge, a fee based on the value of the package contents, you must pick up the package at the post office. If this customs charge must be paid, the post office will send you a notice telling you that you received a package and that you must come to the post office to pick it up. You will have to pay the

Postal abbreviations for U.S. states

AL	Alabama
AK	Alaska
AZ	Arizona
AR	Arkansas
CA	California
CO	Colorado
CT	Connecticut
DE	Delaware
DC	District of Columbia
FL	Florida
GA	Georgia
HI	Hawaii
ID	Idaho
IL	Illinois
IN	Indiana
IA	Iowa
KS	Kansas
KY	Kentucky
LA	Louisiana
ME	Maine
MD	Maryland
MA	Massachusetts
MI	Michigan
MN	Minnesota
MS	Mississippi
MO	Missouri
MT	Montana
NE	Nebraska
NV	Nevada
NH	New Hampshire
NJ	New Jersey
NM	New Mexico
NY	New York
NC	North Carolina
ND	North Dakota
OH	Ohio
OK	Oklahoma
OR	Oregon
PA	Pennsylvania
RI	Rhode Island
SC	South Carolina
SD	South Dakota
TN	Tennessee
TX	Texas
UT	Utah
VT	Vermont
VA	Virginia
WA	Washington
WV	West Virginia
WI	Wisconsin
WY	Wyoming

customs charge at the post office before taking the package.

As in most countries, you do not need to pay a customs charge if a package you receive is a gift. The package you are receiving should be clearly marked by the sender as a gift.

If you want to send a package to another country, take it to the post office. A postal worker will weigh it and charge you postage according to the weight. There is a weight and size limit: it should not weigh more than 45 pounds and its dimensions should not be more than 71 inches. You will not need to open the package and show its contents to the official. You will have to complete a form listing the contents, estimated value, and whether or not it is a gift.

In addition to the U.S. post office, there are private package delivery services. Two of the most popular are UPS (United Parcel Service) and Federal Express. Both can deliver packages to other countries.

Private package delivery services

UPS	412-323-1500
Federal Express	1-800-238-5355

The Internet and E-mail

Throughout the world and especially in the United States, the Internet is becoming a popular way to get and share information. You can use the Internet to send and receive electronic mail also known as e-mail. You might use the Internet at work. University students can usually use computers at school to access the Internet. If you have your own computer, you can get affordable access and an e-mail account through a national or local Internet service provider (ISP). In Allegheny County, you can go to any Carnegie Library and many community libraries to use the Internet for free. The Internet is easy to use and you can ask a librarian for help. The Carnegie Library in Oakland organizes free introduction and Internet research sessions to the general public.

If you decide that you want to use the Internet at home, you will need to consider the expense of buying a computer, the necessary software, equipment, and monthly Internet service provider fees, which typically cost $20 per month. A computer powerful enough to run the correct software and a modem to connect your computer to a telephone line are now more affordable than ever. Some new computers cost less than $1000.

You can find books and magazines about the Internet, and computers in general, at libraries and bookstores.

The **Three Rivers Free Net** (TRFN) provides free dial-in Internet access to computer users who have a modem. The TRFN's Web page has links to many Pittsburgh area organizations as well as information about Pittsburgh including community activities, employment, and Pittsburgh news. You can call them at **412-622-8862**. Their Web address is http://trfn.clpgh.org.

Connecting to the Internet at Home

You can connect to the Internet through an Internet service provider. There are many national and local providers in the Pittsburgh area who offer Internet access, e-mail, and Web page space for about $20 per month. You can contact a service provider by telephone. They will mail you information about what software you need in order to connect your computer.

You can find the names of some Internet service providers in the Yellow Pages telephone book under "Internet Services—Consumer." Service providers also advertise in a local free monthly computer newspaper, *Computer User.* The Three River Free Net's Web page has a complete list of more than 30 local and national Internet service providers available in Pittsburgh.

Media

American businesses are experts at distributing information and marketing products through TV, magazines, newspapers, radio, and other information sources. Advertising and all forms of information distribution are big businesses in the United States. You will never be able to escape advertising for stores, shopping, services, and sports.

Finding good sources of news and other information that interests you can be an overwhelming process. But everything is available if you look for it long and hard enough. Keep in mind that the best information sources, especially for news, are often not the most popular.

Pittsburgh has several newspapers and many TV and radio stations that provide international, national, and local news and information. In general, coverage of international issues throughout the United States is not as extensive as national and local reporting. However, there are some sources for good international news. The *New York Times* and *Wall Street Journal*, both published nationally, offer excellent international news coverage.

The only way to find what you want is to just start looking: turn on the TV, read the newspaper, and listen to the radio.

Newspapers and Magazines

You can buy newspapers at any supermarket, drugstore, bookstore, or newspaper vender downtown. There are also vending boxes on streets where you can buy local newspapers. It is more expensive to buy the newspaper from vending boxes than it is to get it delivered to your home.

The most popular and largest newspaper in Pittsburgh is the *Pittsburgh Post-Gazette*, published seven days a week. It offers good local and national news as well as some international news. The Sunday edition of the *Post-Gazette* is the most popular edition because it has coupons, comics, special sections, and a large classified section for apartments and other real estate, used cars, and other items. You can have the *Post-Gazette* delivered to your home by calling 412-263-1121.

The *Pittsburgh Tribune-Review*, actually published in Greensburg, is another local newspaper. For home delivery, call 800-909-8742.

In addition to these newspapers, there are several free weekly papers. The best among them are *InPittsburgh* and *City Paper*, which have current listings of cultural events that take place in Pittsburgh each week. These are good papers in which to find foreign and American film listings, reviews, music events, art exhibitions, festivals, and restaurants.

Another good source of cultural information for Pittsburgh is *Pittsburgh Magazine*, a monthly magazine that has in-depth articles on local issues as well as good listings of restaurants and shopping information. Every year, *Pittsburgh Magazine* publishes a City Guide that lists restaurants, stores, arts organizations, cinemas, sports teams, and famous sights, among other useful information. You can order a City Guide or subscribe to the magazine by calling 412-622-1360. *Pittsburgh Magazine* is also sold in bookstores.

Among the best places to become familiar with newspapers and magazines is at a bookstore or at the Carnegie Library in Oakland. There you can browse through a variety of magazines and newspapers. The University of Pittsburgh's Hillman Library in Oakland (across from the Carnegie Library) has newspapers and magazines from many other countries. If you want to purchase newspapers and magazines from other countries, try the University Book Center at the University of Pittsburgh, bookstores such as Borders and Barnes & Noble, as well as some newsstands.

Television

Commercial Stations. There are many TV stations in Pittsburgh. Among them, Channels 2, 4, 11, 22, and 53 are local stations with local news broadcasts, each affiliated with one of the major national networks. Commercial stations offer entertainment programs: dramas, comedies, cartoons (animated programs), and daily news broadcasts.

Public Stations. Pittsburgh has one publicly supported TV station, WQED on Channel 13. This is affiliated with the Public Broadcasting System (PBS), a national network of public stations that broadcast fine arts performances, dramas, comedies, and news as well as educational children's programs. These stations are funded by the government and by local yearly contributions.

Cable Television. Cable is a paid service that provides viewers with a wider variety of stations and better reception for both local and cable channels. Cable television can be one of the best sources for international news; look in your local listings for the international channel for international news and other programming in your native language, as well as CNN for summarized international coverage.

Movie Theaters

Our city has a wide variety of movie theaters, both within the city proper and in the outlying suburbs. Most of the multiplexes, or multi-screen theaters, are located outside the city, and are accessible by car. Some small, single screen theaters are the Rex, the Beehive in Oakland, the Regent Square Theater in Regent Square, and the Hollywood in Dormont.

Videos

You can rent videos at video stores as well as at many grocery stores and drug stores. You will most likely have to pay a small fee in order to obtain a membership at one of these stores. The video lending services they provide function the same way as lending library services do; if you borrow a video and keep it too long, you will have to pay a late fee. Many video rental stores have a return box if the store is closed.

If you have brought your VCR, TV, or stereo system with you from your home country, you will not be able to use it without first consulting an electronics company about necessary alterations to your equipment. This company can help you choose the attachments or adaptors you will need to make your equipment functional in the United States. Look in the local Yellow Pages under "Television" or "Stereophonic & High Fidelity Equipment." If you plan to return to your home country within the next several years, please consult with an electronics expert about whether equipment you buy here could be usable in your home country.

Radio

There are dozens of local AM and FM radio stations in Pittsburgh.

Pittsburgh public and university FM radio stations

WRCT (Carnegie Mellon University)	88.3	rock, international
WQED (Public radio)	89.3	classical
WDUQ (Duquesne University)	90.5	jazz, NPR news
WYEP (Independent)	91.3	rock, folk, news
WPTS (University of Pittsburgh)	92.1	rock, international

Most stations on FM play some style of popular music along with brief news broadcasts. Most AM stations broadcast news, talk radio, sports, and popular music.

There are several publicly supported radio stations; some are associated with local universities. Public stations are the only stations that play classical and jazz music in Pittsburgh.

Most radios that you buy in U.S. stores have AM and FM. Some people listen to shortwave radio because foreign services broadcast in foreign languages to North America. Shortwave radios are available at Radio Shack, a store that specializes in radios and electronics.

Money

Cash is issued in $1, $5, $10, $20, $50, and $100 denominations. Most people carry $1, $5, $10, and $20 bills to use when shopping. It can be difficult to get change for a $50 or $100 bill. One dollar is divided into 100 cents. Each coin has a name: penny (1 cent), nickel (5 cents), dime (10 cents), and quarter (25 cents).

Bank Accounts

It is a good idea to establish a bank account at an American bank so you can conveniently write checks and deposit and withdraw money. Checks are useful for paying bills such as your electricity or credit card bill by mail or when you order things by mail. Your bank will also give you an ATM (automated teller machine) or cash machine card to withdraw money at a machine. Your bank can also issue you traveler's checks. You might also be able to get a credit card from your bank.

There are many banks in Pittsburgh. Some banks, such as Mellon Bank and PNC Bank, have offices in other cities. Other banks might only be located in your area. All of them offer the same basic services: savings accounts and checking accounts. A savings account is simply a safe place to keep money. You can deposit and withdraw money. While money is in the account, it earns a small amount of interest. A checking account generally does not earn interest, but you can write checks from this account. Some banks offer checking accounts that pay interest.

Before opening an account, you should compare two or three banks and choose the best one for you. When choosing a bank, there are several things to think about:

- How convenient is the bank's location? Is there a bank near your residence? Most Pittsburgh banks have locations all over the city and suburbs. Some are even located in Giant Eagle supermarkets.

- What is the minimum you have to deposit to open an account?

- What is the minimum you have to keep in your account?

- What does the bank charge for services?

- What penalties does the bank charge for an overdraft or a low account balance?

- How much does it cost to use the ATM (automatic teller machine)?

- What international services do you need? For example, can your bank change and deposit a check from a foreign bank in your American bank account?

To open an account at a bank, call to make an appointment with a bank representative. A representative can help you open a new account as well as answer

How to write a personal check

1. Your address will be printed on this side of your personal bank checks. You will receive these checks approximately one week after you open your account.

2. Write in the month and the day, following this model. Here 8 means August, 12 means the twelfth day of the month, (in the U.S., always record dates listing the month first, followed by the day), and 98 is the year.

3. Write in the full name of the person or company to whom you will send the check. Be sure that this information can be easily read.

4. Preprinted check number.

5. Write in the numerical dollar amount. In the U.S., the use of commas and periods is reversed when compared to usage in many other cultures. Be careful when you write numerical amounts.

6. Write out the full amount of the check, following this model.

7. Preprinted bank address.

8. This area can help you keep track of why you wrote the check.

9. Sign your name here. Checks are not valid without your signature. If you *receive* a check, endorse it by signing in the space provided on the *back* of the check.

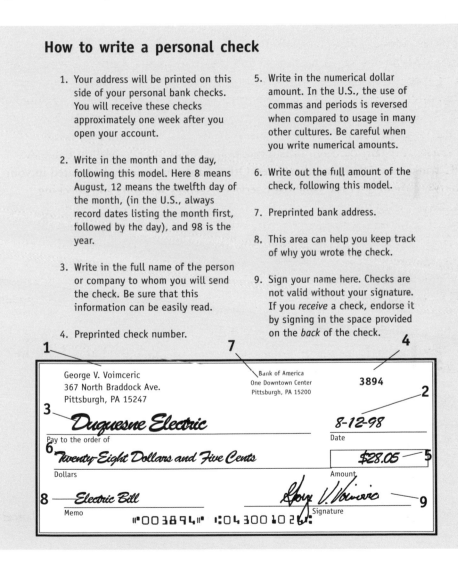

all your questions about services, procedures, and fees. Ask about how to write a check, use an ATM machine, and read and understand a bank statement. You can find the names and phone numbers of local banks in the Yellow Pages or simply walk into a bank.

When you open checking and savings accounts, you will need several pieces of identification as well as enough money in U.S. dollars to make your first deposit. Acceptable identification includes your passport and a Pennsylvania non-driver ID card, Pennsylvania driver's license, or a corporate or student identification card.

ATMs

You can use an ATM (automatic teller machine) or cash machine to make deposits and receive cash from your accounts. ATMs are convenient because you can use them at any time of day or night at many locations. You can find them on the street, in supermarkets, and malls. In this region they are usually identified by signs that say MAC, which stands for Money Access Center.

Your bank will give you an ATM card and a PIN (personal identification) number. A PIN number is a secret number that you memorize and enter into a cash machine. Do not tell others your PIN number. You need to enter your PIN into a cash machine in order to receive cash. Your bank will charge you a small fee each time you use an ATM machine operated by another bank.

Credit Cards

As a newcomer to the United States, you might consider getting a credit card (Master Card, Visa, Discover, American Express). Credit cards are convenient for renting a car and making large purchases such as airplane tickets. Most stores, including large grocery stores, accept credit cards. Your bank is one place to apply for a credit card.

Credit History

When you apply for a credit card, your bank will check your credit history. A credit history is a record of your past loans, credit cards, and banking activity. The purpose of checking your credit history is for the bank to make sure that you are a person who can and will pay a credit card bill every month.

As a newcomer, you might have difficulty getting approved because you might have no credit history in the United States. You will need to provide as much information as possible to your bank about your credit history in your country and employment in the United States to help you get a card.

Currency Exchange

There are no restrictions on the amount of money you can bring in or out of the United States. However, you must register amounts of more than $5,000 with U.S. customs when you enter and leave the country.

Although most banks offer foreign currency services, only Mellon Bank and PNC Bank offer more comprehensive services, such as currency exchange.

Transferral of Funds

This is one service provided by both Mellon Bank and PNC Bank. Through these institutions, you will be able to wire money in and out of the United States. To do this, you might have to pay a transaction fee ranging from $15 to $50. You might also be required to pay a conversion fee (a fee for changing from one currency to another). It is possible that this fee could be included in the exchange rate. Please ask your bank service representative about this fee.

To transfer funds, you will need to know how long the transaction will take and whether the service has pickup and delivery. You must also be able to present necessary information: the names and addresses of your foreign bank and your U.S. bank's main branch, the routing number of each bank, your account number, and identification (passport, driver's license, credit card).

Mellon Bank

You can exchange major currencies in cash at Mellon Bank from 8:30 a.m. to 4:00 p.m., Monday through Friday at their downtown location at Fifth Avenue and Smithfield Street. If you have an account at the bank, you can wire (transfer) money to another country and receive wire transfers. You might also decide to deposit a check from a foreign bank. If this is the case, your bank might charge you a service fee of between $20–$50 per check; keep in mind that this fee will vary. Call 412-234-4215 for information.

PNC Bank

You can also exchange major currencies at PNC Bank downtown at Fifth and Wood Streets from 8:30 a.m. to 3:30 p.m., Monday through Friday. If you have an account at the bank, you can also send and receive wire transfers and change checks. Call 412-762-2090.

Traveler's Checks

If you travel outside the Pittsburgh area and need to carry large amounts of cash, you should buy traveler's checks. Traveler's checks work like cash but are safer to use because you must sign each check twice before you use it. The company from which you buy traveler's checks will also replace them if they are lost or stolen.

You can buy traveler's checks in U.S. dollars at most banks. American Express, Visa, and Thomas Cook are three common, widely recognized traveler's checks that you can buy in banks. You pay a percentage (usually about 2%) as a fee for the checks. Ask a bank teller for information about traveler's checks.

You can also purchase traveler's checks in several foreign currencies at the **American Express** office downtown at 2 PPG Place on Market Square (412-391-3202) and at the American Automobile Association (AAA) office downtown on Smithfield Street under Mellon Square.

Taxes

Everyone in the United States pays taxes. When you buy something in a store, eat in a restaurant, and earn money from your job, you pay taxes. Some taxes, such as sales taxes, are simple to determine. Other taxes, such as income taxes, are often more complicated.

Sales Tax

Every time you buy something in Pennsylvania, you pay a sales tax. Sales tax is determined by the price of an item and added automatically when you pay. For example, if you buy a novel in a bookstore that has a $10 price tag, you will pay an additional $.70 in taxes, or $10.70 total. All items and services are taxed at 7% in Allegheny County, 6% elsewhere in Pennsylvania. You do not pay sales taxes when you buy food and clothing. Food from a restaurant, however, is taxed. Alcohol, cigarettes, rental cars, and hotel stays are taxed at different rates. You also pay a tax when you buy gasoline for your car. Gasoline tax is already added in the price per gallon; the price you see on the pump is the amount you pay the cashier.

Income and Property Taxes

Everyone who works in the United States pays income taxes. Unlike many countries where residents pay national taxes, residents of Pennsylvania (and other states) pay taxes to several levels of government. If you live and work in Allegheny County, you must pay federal, state, local (city or township taxes), and sometimes county taxes.

If you own property, such as your own home, you also pay taxes based on the value of your property.

The process of determining which taxes and how much tax you must pay can be confusing even for longtime local residents. Each level of government has its own rules, forms, tax collection agency, tax collector, or tax office. Each agency taxes only certain kinds of income but more than one might tax the same kind of income. For example, if you live in the City of Pittsburgh, you pay tax based on your work income to the City of Pittsburgh, as well as to the State of Pennsylvania, and to the U.S. Government.

As a new resident or foreign resident, you will likely have a special tax status. The kind of tax and how much you must pay depends on several factors. These factors include: how much money you earn from work, whether or not you own property in the United States, how much money you earn from investments, where you live, and how long you have been living there. Another important factor you must consider is whether or not your home country has a special tax agreement with the United States. This agreement might affect how much you pay for federal taxes. Here is some basic information and advice about paying taxes:

All taxes are due on April 15 following the end of the previous tax year. In other words, you must pay taxes for 1997 (January 1, 1997 to December 31, 1997) on or before April 15, 1998. Taxes paid after this date are late, and you might have to pay a penalty for late taxes.

Take advantage of tax advice provided by your employer. If you have been transferred to the Pittsburgh area by a company, they might be experienced with the federal and local tax status of foreign residents. Ask your director or contact person early on in your stay so that you can plan ahead.

If you are a student, ask your foreign student advisor for advice. He or she might be able to tell you what to do or give you advice about whom to contact.

If you have investments, property, or a high income, you should consider meeting with a tax professional. A professional financial advisor, tax advisor or tax preparer can give you correct advice that can save you time and money.

As April 15 approaches, tax professionals and preparers become busy. Many post offices stay open until midnight on April 15 so that people can mail their tax forms until the last moment. You, however, should not procrastinate. As a foreign resident, you might have to take a lot of time to gather documents, understand directions, locate special information, and prepare forms.

General Tax Terms

Tax Returns. Tax returns are tax forms—the documents you use to determine what kind of tax you must pay and how much. Tax returns explain how to figure out how much you pay. Each tax collecting agency has its own forms. Often, these forms are automatically mailed to your home address. However, you are responsible for getting these forms yourself from each tax collecting agency. This means you might have to contact the federal, state, and local tax agencies and ask them to send you the correct forms.

These tax forms are known as *tax returns* because in some cases, you get money returned to you from a tax collection agency. For example, many people get money back, returned to them, from the federal government each year. How does this happen? Each time an employee gets a paycheck, an amount of money is withheld or deducted and paid to a tax collection agency. Commonly, Pennsylvania and federal taxes are withheld from each paycheck. In effect, employees are paying taxes little by little throughout the year. At the end of the year when employees complete their tax forms, they often find they paid too much to the tax collection agency. The tax agency must return this extra money. The purpose of a tax form is to determine how much you owe or are owed by an agency.

- **Income tax.** Income tax is based on how much money you earn per year. You pay a percentage of your yearly income as taxes. The percentage and amount you pay is determined by following the directions on the federal, state, and local tax forms (the tax returns) you must complete and mail in by April 15.

- **Property Tax.** Property tax is based on the value of your property, such as the house you own. If you rent a house or apartment, you do not have to pay property tax.

- **Federal Tax.** You pay income taxes to the Internal Revenue Service (IRS), the U.S. Government agency that collects federal taxes. Employers often withhold a certain amount from your paycheck and pay it directly to the IRS.

- **State Tax.** The State of Pennsylvania collects income tax determined by following the directions on your state tax forms.

- **Local Tax.** Local tax is based on your income. You pay local tax to the city or township (suburb) where you live.

- **School Tax.** Money collected for school taxes supports local public schools. Depending on how your municipality is organized, it will collect school taxes through property or income taxes.

- **Social Security Tax.** This tax is also known as FICA (Federal Insurance Contribution Act). If your country has a tax agreement with the United States or if you are a student, you might not have to pay this tax. Otherwise, this tax is withheld from each paycheck.

- **Occupational Privilege Tax.** In some areas, such as the City of Pittsburgh, you pay a one-time tax when you begin working. Each time you get another job, you pay this tax. This tax is usually automatically withheld from your first paycheck.

The tax information, general advice, and terms in this section of the guide give only basic information about paying taxes in the United States. It is important for you to understand that each case is often special, especially if you have a high income and investments.

You should get professional advice when appropriate. Get tax information directly from the IRS, State of Pennsylvania, and your local tax office.

Tax Resources and Information

For information about Federal Taxes, contact the **Internal Revenue Service** (IRS). You can order special instruction booklets and tax forms from IRS Publications and Forms Ordering at **1-800-829-3676**. You can also pick up tax forms and booklets downtown on the first floor of the Federal Building at 1000 Liberty Avenue. As April 15 approaches, some tax forms are available in Carnegie Libraries.

For free tax advice and help completing your tax return, call **Volunteer Income Tax Assistance** (VITA) at **412-281-0112**.

Here are some booklets from the IRS you might need:

- Pub 54 *Tax Guide for U.S. Citizens and Resident Aliens Abroad*
- Pub 513 *Tax Information for Visitors to the United States*
- Pub 515 *Withholding for Tax on Nonresident Aliens and Foreign Companies*
- Pub 519 *U.S. Tax Guide for Aliens*

State of Pennsylvania

You can get free tax advice to help you with your Pennsylvania taxes from **Taxpayer Information and Assistance** at **412-565-7540**.

Call **Forms Ordering** at **1-800-362-2050** for Pennsylvania tax forms.

City of Pittsburgh

For income tax information call **412-255-2511**. If you need to order forms, call **412-255-2524**.

Other Areas

You can find the telephone numbers of your township or suburban tax collecting agency in both the White and Yellow Pages telephone books. Look in the blue section of each book under "Government Offices—City, Borough, Township." Some local governments have a separate tax office with a telephone number. If you cannot find a separate tax office listed for your area, call the general office telephone number.

Tipping

Giving tips, a little extra money, to someone who performs a service is common in many countries. Americans follow a tipping etiquette—unwritten rules about when and how much they tip.

Tipping in the United

People You Should Tip	Amount
Waiters and Waitresses	15% to 20%
Taxi Drivers	15% to 20%
Barbers and Hair Stylists	10% to 15%, or at least $1
Coat checkers	At least $1 per item
Porters	Fixed fee—usually $.50 to $1
Room Service	20%
Hotel Maid	$1 per day
Paper Carrier	$1 per week, or $.25 per day

People You Should Not Tip

Airline stewards, train conductors, bus drivers, and ticket agents
Elevator operators
Gas station attendants
Government employees (customs agents, police, firefighters)
Hotel receptionists
Store clerks
Theater or cinema ushers
Fast food restaurant staff

States is based on two main ideas. First, Americans tip because they understand that a service person's earnings come partly from tipping. Waiters, for example, are paid little because they expect to make money from tips. Second, a tip is a reward for good service. Americans always tip a certain minimum for some services, but will add even more for exceptional service.

Bribes

Bribes and tips are different. A tip is a reward for one of the specific services listed above. A tip is paid after the service has been performed. In theory, it does not have to be paid at all. Bribery, however, is intended to help influence someone such as an official to overlook a violation or a business partner to agree to a deal.

In both the official and informal areas of American society, bribes are completely inappropriate and illegal.

Home

Searching for a place to live is one of the biggest and most important steps you will take during your stay in the United States. As a foreign newcomer, you might find that this is time consuming and difficult. However, this process deserves careful consideration about what you want in a home and a community.

Renting

The more you are able to pay for monthly rent, the more choices you will have. However, rents in Pittsburgh are reasonable compared to many other cities. It is possible to find a nice place to live for an affordable price.

A house or apartment's rent is determined by its size, condition, and especially its location. Some neighborhoods in the city and suburbs are more desirable than others in terms of building quality, neighborhood aesthetics, schools, and proximity to work centers or shopping.

If you choose to live in the suburbs, you will probably need a car to go shopping, get to work, and travel around town. Public transportation is available and efficiently serves commuters going downtown in the morning and returning in the evening but can be less convenient for short trips around town.

As you look, you will probably visit many beautiful houses and apartments as well as some places that do not seem so nice. Do not be discouraged, this is part of the process. The more you look, the more you learn about the city and the kinds of places available. More importantly, you will gain a clearer idea of what you want.

Looking for an apartment

The best place to begin looking for an apartment is in local newspapers, in the classified ad (advertisement) section, also called the apartment listings. Classified ad sections list apartments for rent by direction (North, South, East, and West) and by neighborhood. Ads provide basic information about an advertised apartment:

- Its size, usually expressed as the number of bedrooms (often abbreviated as "Br")
- Monthly rent
- Which utilities (electricity, water, gas, heat) are included in the rent and which you must pay
- The apartment owner's or manager's phone number
- The apartment's location

Some of the best places to find apartment ads are in the *Pittsburgh Post-Gazette* the *Pittsburgh Tribune-Review*, and the free weekly newspapers such as *InPittsburgh* and *City Paper*. You can also walk or drive around a neighborhood to look for Apartment for Rent signs on buildings.

Special Services

Real Estate Companies. Real estate companies often keep lists of available apartments and houses. When you call, they can tell you about several available apartments or homes and refer you to the building's owner. This is a quick way to find out about several places and begin your search.

Management Companies. Management companies are in charge of running apartments. When you call, they will tell you about available apartments or homes and offer to show them to you.

Relocation Services. Relocation services provide comprehensive services in helping you find a place to live. They can help make finding a place to live and settling into life in Pittsburgh easier, especially for families. When you contact a relocation service, a relocation consultant will consider factors such as how much you can pay to rent a home and the size of home you need. They are also knowledgeable about real estate services if you want to buy a home. A relocation consultant can tell you about local neighborhoods, schools, community organizations, and volunteer opportunities. There is sometimes a charge for consulting services.

City Source Associates provides comprehensive relocation consulting services. Consultants are knowledgeable about school districts, neighborhoods, real estate services, renting, and community groups. They offer guided city and regional tours. Contact them at 213 Smithfield Street, (303 Pitt Building, downtown), **412-391-1850.**

Getting to the Point is a relocation service experienced in helping professionals and families make a smooth transition to living in Pittsburgh. Relocation consultants have information about local school districts, neighborhoods, and work opportunities for foreigners. They offer guided tours. Contact them at 6820 Edgerton Avenue, Pittsburgh, PA 15208, **412-362-3363.**

You can find the names of real estate and management companies, relocation services, and apartment services in the Yellow Pages under "Apartments."

Visiting Apartments

After you have found a potential apartment, make an appointment with the landlord (apartment owner) or a rental agent to visit the apartment. Visiting apartments is your opportunity to see what the apartment looks like, ask questions about rent and utilities, and visit the neighborhood. The most important question is: *Do I want to live here?*

Make sure you ask some other important questions and get clear answers.

Do not agree to move into an apartment until the landlord has agreed to repair and clean the apartment and you are satisfied. Landlords who maintain their apartments well are more likely to make repairs on time and treat you honestly.

When you visit an

Questions to ask about an apartment

- How much is the rent?
- How long is the lease?
- How much is the security deposit?
- Who pays for utilities? Which ones must you (the tenant) pay? Which ones must the landlord pay?
- If something needs to be repaired, who will repair it and who must pay for it?
- Is parking available?
- Are laundry facilities available in the building?
- Is anything broken? Do the refrigerator and stove work?
- Is the apartment clean? Is the carpet clean? Does the refrigerator smell?
- Is it secure? Do all windows and doors have good locks?

apartment, you are not required to make a decision. At the end of a visit simply tell the landlord that you want to think about it. You should visit several apartments before deciding. You might want to learn more about what is available, talk with different landlords, and ask questions. When you find an apartment and want to move in, call the landlord back. Then you can move on to the next step.

When you tell a landlord that you want to move in, he or she might want to perform a credit check. The purpose of this check is to see if you are a trustworthy person who will pay rent on time each month. However, as a newcomer, you likely will not have a credit history. You will need to provide some other documents from your school, job, or bank to show that you will be able to pay rent. Some landlords might be unwilling to accept tenants who do not have a credit history.

Leases

A lease is a written and legal contract between a landlord and a tenant (you). It describes the restrictions and responsibilities of the tenant and the landlord. Carefully read and make sure you understand the lease before you sign it. When you sign the lease, you have made a real commitment to living in the apartment.

Security Deposits

A landlord usually requires a security deposit—money in addition to the rent that you must pay when you sign the lease. Landlords collect security deposits in order to protect themselves from paying for any exceptional damage that you might cause to the apartment. If there is no unusual damage to the apartment, your landlord must return your security deposit when your lease expires and you move out. Typically, a security deposit equals one month's rent. By law it cannot equal more than two months' rent. When you pay your security deposit, pay by check and get a receipt for the money.

In the second year of a lease, the landlord might keep no more than one month's rent as a security deposit. Security deposits of more than $100 must be deposited in a bank. After your third year in an apartment, your landlord must put the security deposit in an interest-bearing account and pay you the interest earned when he or she returns the money.

When you move out, the landlord must either return your entire security deposit or give you a list of any damages and their repair costs. Your landlord must do this in 30 days. If the landlord does not do this, he or she must return your entire deposit.

Location

One of the most important considerations in choosing a place to live is its location.

Typical information on a lease

- How much you will pay for rent and for the security deposit.

- Who pays utilities.

- Occupancy limit.

- Whether pets are allowed.

- How long the rental period is. Typical leases require at least one year but you can discuss this with your prospective landlord before you sign.

- Penalties for breaking the lease. This is how much you would have to pay if you moved out of the apartment before the lease period expires.

Choosing a location

- If you do not have a washing machine, will you be near a laundromat?

- Is there a supermarket or grocery store nearby?

- If you do not have a car, is there frequent bus service?

- Is there easy access to downtown, your job, and shopping?

This factor might be less important if you are not married and do not have children. However, if you have children, keep in mind that where you live determines where your children go to school. The location of an apartment or house also determines the rent. Desirable neighborhoods tend to have higher rents than less desirable neighborhoods. When you explore a potential neighborhood or suburb, consider other factors that might affect your long-term happiness.

When choosing a neighborhood, you will also want to consider how safe it is—try to find out something about its crime rate. This can be difficult to do. Pittsburgh, like any American city, has safer "desirable" sections and less safe "undesirable" areas. The fact is that although you should avoid some areas, other neighborhoods have a bad reputation that they do not deserve. Many neighborhoods are improving; they are in transition. You will likely find cheaper rents for nice places in these neighborhoods.

Tenant Services

The **Allegheny County Health Department** oversees living conditions in apartments and houses in Allegheny County. You can call this number to report landlords who do not maintain safe housing conditions or do not make needed repairs on time. Call **412-687-2243**.

Neighborhood Legal Services provides legal services to low-income Pittsburgh area residents. In addition to other issues, they do handle some housing related problems such as evictions, discrimination, and utility cut-offs (utility termination). Call **412-255-6700**.

Utilities

When you get an apartment, you will need to make arrangements for basic utilities: gas, electricity, and telephone. You might also want to arrange for cable TV. Some of these services might have already been arranged by your landlord.

Arranging these services is fairly easy. They are available everywhere in Pittsburgh and are not too expensive. The only difficulty in setting up basic utilities is choosing which company to use. Until recently there was only one electric company, one gas company, and one phone company. However, because competition has been permitted, more and more companies are able to provide services. In general, the services that each company provides will be more or less the same.

In many cases, your landlord can tell you which companies provide utility service to your apartment.

Natural Gas

Several companies provide natural gas service in Pittsburgh. You might need natural gas for cooking and heat in winter. Which company you must use depends on where you live. In most cases only one

Gas companies

Equitable Gas	412-442-3050 or 1-800-654-6335
Peoples Natural Gas Co.	412-244-2626 or 1-800-764-0111
Columbia Gas of PA, Inc.	1-888-460-4332
Carnegie Natural Gas Co.	412-655-8630
Apollo Gas Co.	412-655-8510
T.W. Philips Gas and Oil Co.	1-800-222-5101

company serves your house or building. Ask your landlord for the name of the company.

When you get the name of the company, call to establish service. They will ask for your address as well as for identification. The company will make an appointment to come to your house to turn on the gas. In most cases, you must be at your home to meet the representative from the gas company.

Electricity

Electricity for the Pittsburgh area is currently supplied by two companies (this might soon change with the coming of greater

Electric companies

Duquesne Light Co.	412-393-7100
Allegheny Power Co.	1-800-255-3443

competition). The two companies are Duquesne Light and Allegheny Power. Where you live determines which company supplies your electricity.

When you call one of the companies, a customer service representative will ask for your name and address. They will probably require you to come to one of their offices with two pieces of identification to arrange service. You will have to make an appointment for a representative to come to your home to start your service.

Telephone Service

Local Service

Bell Atlantic provides local phone service in the Pittsburgh area. To establish phone service, call **1-800-660-2215** (English) or **1-800-479-0305** (Spanish).

When you call, a customer service representative will explain to you how to get phone service. Expect to wait a few minutes before you can talk to a person. You will have to go through a phone menu and wait for a representative.

The representative will ask you for your address and ask you to fax them a copy of your passport for identification. He or she will also explain the different services and prices. It costs approximately $40 to establish phone service in addition to about $16 per month for basic phone service. You will need to spend about 25 minutes on the phone with the operator setting up phone service. It can take three to five days before they give you a telephone number and you can make and receive calls.

The telephone company will send you a phone bill that will tell you how much you must pay for your phone service. You can send payment to the telephone company by check.

Soon after you get your local phone service, Bell Atlantic will send you two phone books that you should keep to use for reference.

The White Pages is published yearly and lists all of Bell Atlantic's customers (just about everyone who has a phone in the Pittsburgh area) with their phone numbers. It also has a list of emergency phone numbers as well as government and social service phone numbers. The White Pages explain how to make international phone calls. There is a list of country codes in the front of the book. If you get a telephone number after the White Pages has been published, your telephone number will not be published until the next year.

The Yellow Pages is a useful directory of businesses and services for Pittsburgh. The Yellow Pages is organized alphabetically by category. Most businesses advertise and have phone numbers in the Yellow Pages. It is a great source when you want to find such businesses as mechanics, furniture stores, car dealers, toy stores, and so on.

Long Distance Telephone Service

When you call Bell Atlantic to set up phone service, the customer service representative will ask you which long distance carrier (long distance phone service) you want to use to make calls outside of Bell Atlantic's area. Long distance service allows you to make international calls. Because of competition, there are hundreds of long distance companies for Pittsburgh.

When you first get phone service, you probably will not know which company to use. To start, choose one of the well-known services and then find a cheaper, better one later. Some long distance companies might offer special, cheap rates to your home country. The three largest carriers are AT&T, MCI, and Sprint.

Long distance providers	
AT&T	1-800-222-0300
MCI	1-800-TALK-MCI
Sprint	1-800-767-7759

Making phone calls

With the exception of special three-digit emergency phone numbers (such as 911), standard U.S. telephone numbers are seven digits long, plus a three-digit area code, for example, 412-555-3815. When making local calls, one usually doesn't have to dial the area code. However, in some major cities telephone companies have added additional area codes and require the use of area codes when dialing other vicinities even if they are nearby. Most of Pittsburgh still has one area code, and you will be able to make calls without having to dial an area code. Callers will have to use a new area code (724) to call nearby areas, such as Greensburg and the North Hills, that no longer have the same area code as Pittsburgh.

Long distance calls require the seven-digit number, plus the three-digit area code, plus a 1. For example, 1-212-555-9956.

Toll-free numbers use 800 or 888 in the sequence of numbers. For example, 1-800-555-1900.

International calls require additional country codes. Check your White Pages phone book for a listing of these.

Beware of phone numbers with 900s in them. These numbers make the persons placing the call pay additional money to the person or company that owns the number. These numbers are often used as unscrupulous profit-making tools. You can ask the telephone company to block them from your phone when you sign up for phone service.

Pay phones accept coins, usually requiring 35 cents to make local calls. Very few accept phone "cards" that are common in other countries. However, you might see advertisements for phone cards in stores. You do not insert these cards into pay phones. Instead, by purchasing one you have prepaid for long-distance time, which you access by calling a number printed on the phone card, and then dialing the phone number you wish to call. Sometimes these cards offer good rates, sometimes they do not. Your long distance provider might also give you a "calling card." Similar to the other prepaid phone cards, you dial a number printed on the card and then the number you wish to call. But instead of prepaid time, the cost of the call is billed to your home phone number.

Cable TV

If you own a TV, you might want to consider cable TV service. Cable TV is a monthly service that provides you with access to TV channels. The cable carries TV signals for local, national, special, and sometimes international TV stations. While you do not need cable to receive Pittsburgh's local TV channels (2, 4, 11, 13, etc.), you might receive them better with cable service.

There are many cable companies in the Pittsburgh area. For the moment, each area is served by only one company. Which company you might use depends on where you live. You can find the names and phone numbers of cable companies in your Yellow Pages under "Television—Cable."

When you call the cable company, a customer service representative will explain everything you need to know about setting up cable service. There are several levels of service depending on how many and which channels you want. Prices vary depending which service you choose. The representative will explain the services, monthly costs, installation fee, and activation fee. You might not have to pay for an installation fee if a cable already exists from a previous owner in your home.

Transportation

There are several ways to travel in the United States. To some extent, where you want to go determines how you travel.

Travel here is dominated by cars and airplanes. If you want to travel in the country or to a small or medium-sized town, you will probably have to use a car. Highways connect every city and town. Most cities, even small ones, have an airport. In some cases, however, travel by train or bus is a convenient and inexpensive option.

Airplane

If you want to travel from the east coast to the west coast, an airplane is the only quick option. From Pittsburgh, you can travel to most American cities by plane. There is also direct service to some Canadian and European cities. Pittsburgh International Airport is among the busiest in the United States. A major airline, US Airways (formerly USAir) uses Pittsburgh as a base.

The best way to get tickets is to call an airline directly or talk to a travel agent. Travel agents can sometimes find good ticket prices, especially if you make plans early. In general, ticket prices are lower if you make reservations 21 days in advance. Most travel agents can find good prices to North American, Western European, and Asian cities. For travel to some places, it is best to find an agent who specializes in unusual destinations. You can find travel agencies in the Yellow Pages under "Travel."

When you travel by plane, consider how you will get to and from the airport. Most airports around the country are connected to downtown areas by major highways. Some cities have good public transportation connecting their downtown areas to their airports. You can travel to Pittsburgh's airport by public transportation on the 28X airport shuttle. (Call 412-422-2000 for information.) You can also travel by taxi or in a shuttle van run by a private company. Private shuttle vans usually leave for the airport from major hotels. You can find private van transportation in the Yellow Pages under "Airport Transportation."

Allow yourself two extra hours at the airport before your flight for security checks and processing.

Train

Train travel is often overlooked, but is worth your time to explore. It takes longer to reach your destination than by air and passenger service is not as extensive as that in many other countries, but it can cost less than plane travel. For many people, traveling by train is much more enjoyable and convenient. It is one of the best ways to see the country. Most train stations are located in downtown areas of cities.

Passenger trains are run by **Amtrak**, the national train company. Pittsburgh's train station is located downtown at 1100 Liberty Avenue below The Pennsylvanian apartment building, across from the Greyhound bus station. You can call **1-800-872-7245** to ask about train schedules and make reservations. Service to Chicago, Philadelphia, New York, and Washington is good. It is also possible to travel across the country even to some Canadian cities by train.

Bus

In addition to train travel, buses offer service to many cities. Service is cheaper and sometimes faster than by train. Service to Washington, DC, for example, is direct, fast, and inexpensive.

Greyhound, a national bus company, offers service throughout the United States. The bus station is located at 11th Street and Liberty Avenue downtown. Call **1-800-231-2222** (in English) and **1-800-531-5332** (in Spanish) to ask about schedules and prices.

Rental Car

If you want to travel to small towns or if you want complete flexibility when you travel, you can rent a car. There are many places to rent a car in Pittsburgh. When you rent a car, call several car rental agencies and compare daily and weekly prices as well as service. Rental agencies require you to give them your credit card number or leave a cash deposit when you rent a car. If you leave a cash deposit, you get the deposit back when you return the car. Most Americans use a credit card to rent cars. You can find the names of car rental agencies in the Yellow Pages telephone book under "Automobile Renting."

Some car rental companies require you to be at least 25 years of age and to own your own car. Others charge an extra fee for drivers under 25. Car rental companies will require an international permit and/or a driver's license from your country.

Make sure you ask these questions:

- How much does it cost to rent per day and per week?
- Is there unlimited mileage? If not, what is the mileage limit?
- What should you do if the car breaks down and needs to be repaired? Does the rental company have a 24-hour emergency phone number?

Private Car

If you own a car, you can go anywhere. Gasoline prices in the United States are among the cheapest in the world. If you plan to travel to another city by car, get a good map that shows highways and roads. You can buy a U.S. road atlas (a book of maps) at bookstores. If you are a member of the AAA, you get free maps to your destination as part of your yearly membership.

Driving

Depending on how people drive in your country, you might find driving here easy and orderly. Most drivers follow the rules: they respect signs, stay under the speed limit, and are usually courteous to other drivers. Signs and stop lights are generally easy to see.

Driver's Licenses

Licenses for cars and trucks in Pennsylvania are regulated by the **Pennsylvania Department of Transportation**, commonly known as PennDOT. Their main office is in Harrisburg, Pennsylvania's capital. Call PennDOT at **1-800-932-4600** if you have questions about your driver's license, or about taking a driving test. You can also obtain information on the phone about office locations.

You can use a driver's license from another country with an International Driving Permit for up to one year. When your foreign license or the international permit expires, you must apply for a Pennsylvania license. You must give up your foreign license and international permit when you apply for a Pennsylvania license. Pennsylvania allows you to have only one valid driver's license at a time. Foreign language documents that you must take with you when you apply for a license must be translated into English by a certified translator. The translation must be notarized and must include a copy of the translator's certification.

Notaries

For some official documents, including those involving driving, you must have an authorized person, a notary, verify that you are the person named in a document. Notaries are certified by the state and provide their service to the public, usually for a small fee. In order to have a document notarized, take it to a notary. He or she will put a seal on the document, notarizing the document. You can find notaries in real estate, insurance offices, and at car dealers. A notary can also help you register your car. There is a list of notaries in the Yellow Pages under "Notaries."

Getting a Pennsylvania driver's license

1. Get a copy of the *Pennsylvania Motor Vehicles Rule Book*. This book explains all the rules for driving in Pennsylvania. The manual is only available in English and Spanish. You should read the entire book because you will have to take a short test to see if you know the rules. You can get a copy of the *Rule Book* at the **Western Pennsylvania Motor Club**, 202 Penn Circle West (**412-362-3300**) and at the State Police Barracks on Washington Boulevard (**412-645-7492**). Or you can call PennDOT to have a copy mailed to you.

2. Bring your birth certificate or your passport when you go to apply for your license. Also bring your driver's license from home. Go to the State Police Barracks on Washington Boulevard to take a brief test on driving rules and signs in Pennsylvania. (Call PennDot for other locations). You must also take an eye exam there. Unless this is your first driver's license, you do not need to take and pass the driving test in a car.

3. If you pass the brief test on rules, you can get a temporary driver's license for $24. You can drive with this license for 60 days. You will also get an application for a regular driver's license, which you must fill out and send to PennDOT (the address is on the application). After you send in the application, you will receive a "camera card" in the mail within 60 days.

4. When you receive the camera card, take it to a Photo License Center. Your camera card will have a list of Photo License Centers including addresses and phone numbers. Also take identification such as your passport. Your photograph will be taken, and you will be given an official Pennsylvania driver's license.

Your Pennsylvania license is valid in any state. Each state has its own driving rules but, in general, they are similar. If you learn to drive well in Pittsburgh, you are probably ready to drive anywhere.

Buying a Car

If you decide to buy a car, the first thing you must decide is whether you want a new or used car. Both are easily available. Your main consideration will be how much money you can spend. No matter what kind of car you want, expect to spend a lot of time looking and test driving cars. Because there are so many available, find one that you like and that you can afford.

Buying a car, new or used, is one of the few situations in the United States when you can bargain for a good price.

New Cars. There are new car dealers everywhere in the Pittsburgh area. The best place to start looking for a new car is in the Yellow Pages under "Automobile Dealers" where you can find the names, locations, and phone numbers of car dealers. In general, new cars will have a warranty (a written guarantee) that pays for most repairs. You should read and make sure you understand the warranty. Take your time looking at a new car, feel free to ask questions, and test drive the car. Do not allow the dealer to pressure you into making a decision.

Used Cars. There are many used cars available. Prices vary according to the age, mileage, type, and condition of the car. If you are persistent and spend a lot of time looking, you can find a good car at a good price. Used cars are sold by individuals and by car dealers. The best place to look for a used car is in the newspaper classified advertisements section. There are also free booklets, such as *Motor Mart* or *Auto Mart,* that list used cars for sale, often with a photograph of the car. You can find free booklets at supermarkets or drugstores.

Most used cars do not come with any kind of warranty. When you buy a used car you buy it as is: as soon as you pay the money, you cannot return the car. Be sure to inspect the car and test drive it. Most people who want to buy a used car spend a lot of time making phone calls and going to look at different cars before choosing.

License Plates and Car Registration

You must have a license plate in order to drive your car legally. A license plate is a metal plate with numbers issued by PennDOT that identifies your car.

Getting a license plate and registering a car for the first time can be a complicated process. You need to have a driver's license, several documents such as the title, and proof of insurance. The title is a document that proves you are the owner of the car. You will also have to pay several processing fees. What you must do to get a license plate depends on where you bought your car.

If you buy a new or used car from a dealer, they will be able to tell you what you need and facilitate the process for you. If you buy a used car from an individual, you should contact a notary or messenger service that specializes in getting license plates. You can find messenger services in the Yellow Pages under "Messenger Services."

If you buy a car, you must register it with PennDOT for $36 each year. When you register your car, PennDOT will send you a car registration card. This is a document that proves your car is registered with the state. You should keep this with you when you drive. PennDOT will also send you a registration sticker to put on the license plate of your car.

Inspection

You must have your car inspected for safety and exhaust emissions (pollution control) once a year. You can have your car inspected by any certified mechanic. Authorized mechanics have an official sign in the garage that states they are certified by PennDOT to inspect cars. If your car passes these tests, the mechanic will put an inspection sticker in the front windshield of your car. The inspection is good for one year. The sticker has a date that tells you when you have to have your car inspected again. If you do not have a valid sticker, the police can give you a ticket.

Car Insurance

In Pennsylvania, you must have minimum liability insurance coverage. Liability insurance pays for damages caused to other people when an accident is your fault. The absolute minimum is $15,000 per person to pay other persons hurt in an accident, $30,000 per accident.

However, most car owners have more liability insurance coverage. The amount you will have for your car is sometimes determined by who is financing your car. In other words, the bank where you received your car loan or the company providing the payment plan for your car will have different, usually higher insurance requirements.

You buy car insurance from an insurance company. You should contact several companies and talk with an insurance agent about costs, kinds of insurance, and level of coverage. There are several kinds of coverage. You do not need all of them. You only need the kind and level appropriate for the make, age, and value of your car.

You can find insurance companies in the Yellow Pages telephone book under "Insurance." Some kinds of insurance you might consider:

- **Collision insurance**: pays for damage to your car if it is in an accident.
- **Comprehensive insurance**: pays for damages and loss from theft or vandalism.

Car Accidents

If you have an accident while driving, you must stop. Do not drive away. If you drive away from an accident, the police will charge you with hit and run, a crime in Pennsylvania and the United States.

If you have an accident, it is your responsibility to get specific information from the other driver. You must also give certain information to the other driver. The purpose of this information is for your insurance company

If you have a car accident . . .

- Write down the name, full address, home and work phone number of the other driver in the accident.

- Write down the insurance company name, phone number, and car insurance policy number of the other driver.

- Write down the license plate number of the other car in the accident.

- Write a description of the damage, where the accident happened, and how it happened.

- If possible, take a photograph of the damage.

- Call your insurance company immediately and report the accident.

(and the other driver's insurance company) to decide who is responsible for causing the accident and who (usually an insurance company) must pay for damages.

In Pittsburgh, police will not come to the scene of an accident unless someone is injured or a car cannot be driven away.

Alcohol and Driving

Driving while drunk or under the influence of alcohol (DUI) is a crime in the United States. Police everywhere are generally strict about stopping and checking drivers they think might be drunk. According to Pennsylvania law, you are considered to be driving under the influence or DUI if the level of alcohol in your blood is .10% or higher (a person who weighs 120 pounds will measure .10% after three beers, three glasses of wine, or three shots of liquor).

If the police stop you because they think you are DUI, they will give you a breath, blood, or urine test to measure the level of alcohol in your blood. The penalties are strict: you can lose your driver's license for up to one year as well as spend time in jail and have to pay a fine.

It is illegal to drink alcohol or have an open container of alcohol in your car while driving.

Driving in Pittsburgh

Weather. The weather affects how people drive. The weather changes from day to day, especially during the winter. Driving in dry, clear weather is different from driving in wet and snowy weather. When there is heavy rain and snow, most drivers slow down. In wet weather, drive slower and expect to take longer to go where you want to go. Be especially cautious when driving down Pittsburgh's steep hills in the snow. It is easy to slide and have an accident.

If you have never driven in winter weather, be aware that you must drive differently in order to accommodate slippery conditions. For example, when driving on snow-covered roads, do not brake suddenly and hard. This will cause your car to slide, and you will lose control of your vehicle.

Winter weather might slow down drivers, but it generally does not stop people from going about their day. People are used to driving in bad weather. They just expect to spend more time traveling. Trucks clear away snow and pour road salt on streets to melt ice and snow. Most Americans buy special snow tires for driving on snow and ice covered roads. People also buy scrapers for removing ice from car windows. They keep road salt or sand in the trunks of their cars to put on snow or ice when they get stuck.

The most serious damage caused by winter weather is to streets and cars. The road salt put on streets causes car bodies to erode and rust. Freezing and thawing is the major cause of potholes, the holes and bumps you will find on many streets in Pittsburgh.

Speeding. Most drivers follow the speed limits posted on the streets. There are exceptions. On some streets and roads, all drivers go faster than the speed limit because they think the limits are too low. On Routes 376 and 279, many drivers will go about five miles faster than the limit. Sometimes the police stop speeding drivers and sometimes not. Keep in mind that the police can stop you if you are even slightly over the speed limit and probably will give you an expensive speeding ticket. It is safest not to drive faster than the speed limit.

Stop Lights. You should always stop at a red light and slow down for a yellow light. After driving for a short time in Pittsburgh, you will notice that many drivers speed up when they see a yellow light so that they will not have to stop for the red light that will come soon after. It is recommended that you slow down and stop completely at yellow lights.

Stop Signs. According to the law, you must stop fully at a stop sign. The police can give you a ticket you if you only slow down.

Pedestrians. Pedestrians have the right of way at all times. You must stop to let people cross the street if they are walking in the street. This is especially important if there is a cross walk—two white lines painted across the street.

Miles. Americans use miles not kilometers to measure large distances. A mile is longer than a kilometer, 1 km = .6 miles. Speed limits and distances on road signs are described in terms of miles. A "Speed Limit 55" sign means miles per hour or MPH. This might seem slow in terms of kilometers but not in miles.

Turns. You may make a right turn when the light is red, unless a sign says, "No Turn On Red." Stop and look for oncoming traffic before you turn. At intersections, the driver who arrives first goes through first, and others must take their turns.

Tunnels. When you drive through the Squirrel Hill or Fort Pitt Tunnels, you will notice that drivers often reduce their speeds. This causes traffic delays, especially when people are driving to and from work.

Parking

Depending on where you live and work, parking your car will be difficult or easy. In some popular areas of the city, it can be difficult to find a parking space, such as downtown and in Oakland near the universities. Of course, there are many private parking lots and parking garages that charge a fee for parking. There are also several kinds of public parking spaces:

Metered Parking. On many streets you will find parking meters. These generally cost $.25 per half hour. Some meters give you fifteen minutes, others give you an hour. If your time expires and you do not add more money, you can get a parking ticket that costs at least $10.

Free Street Parking. In most neighborhoods, you can park for free on the streets. Before you park on a street, look for signs that limit parking. Yellow paint on the curb means no parking. You cannot park in front of a fire hydrant. Parking is sometimes not allowed on one side of the street each month to allow street cleaning.

Permit Parking. In some neighborhoods, street parking is limited to one hour except for residents who have a permit parking sticker in the windshield of their car. A parking permit allows you to park in a certain area for an unlimited amount of time. You can park only on streets authorized by your permit. For example, if you have a permit with the letter *J* you can only park on streets with signs that allow permits with the letter *J*. Dormont, Shadyside, and many other neighborhoods require permits for parking. Check with your local police.

You can get a permit parking sticker downtown at 232 Boulevard of the Allies (412-560-2500). When you apply for permit parking, bring your driver's license, car registration, and a copy of your apartment lease as well as $20 for the yearly fee.

Handicapped Parking. You might notice that there are often free spaces near the entrances to supermarkets, office buildings, and in shopping centers. If these spaces have a large, blue wheelchair sign, they are reserved for handicapped drivers. Do not park in these spaces! Handicapped drivers have either handicapped license plates or official signs in their cars. If you park in a handicapped space but are not handicapped, you might have to pay a $227 parking ticket.

Parking Chairs. Because there is little parking in some city neighborhoods, residents have made their own rules. In some neighborhoods where all parking is unlimited and free, residents claim parking spaces by putting chairs in street parking spaces. Other residents expect the space directly in front of their house to remain free. Do not be surprised if someone asks you to move from a space in front of their house—they consider that space their own. Never move a chair from a parking space!

Seat Belts and Child Seats

In Pennsylvania, all drivers and passengers in the front seat must wear seat belts. If you have a child under four years of age you must put him or her in a special child safety seat that is approved by the federal government. You should put the safety seat in the back seat of your car. Do not put the safety seat in the front seat, especially if you have an air bag on the passenger side of your car.

You can buy an approved child safety seat at large toy stores and department stores. Fisher Price, Century, and Evenflo are among companies that make approved safety seats. Call 1-800-227-2358 for information about safety seats and child safety in cars.

Repairs

Sooner or later you will need to have your car repaired by a mechanic. Car mechanics experienced at working on most kinds of cars are easy to find in Pittsburgh. If you have a less common car such as a Fiat or Peugeot, you should find a mechanic who specializes in foreign cars.

The best way to find a good car mechanic is to ask for a recommendation from someone else who has a car. If you bought a new car, you probably have a warranty for most repairs and should call the car dealer where you bought the car when there is a problem.

The easiest place to find a mechanic is in the Yellow Pages under "Automobile Repairing and Service." If you are a member of AAA, call them. They can tell you about a mechanic who they recommend.

The **American Automobile Association** (AAA) is a large, national association of drivers and car owners that provides many travel and car related services. If you own a car or are planning to buy a car, you should consider joining AAA as a member. Some of the services they provide are similar to a travel agency.

Among the services they offer members are free maps, emergency repair service all across the country, advice on buying a car, and finding different kinds of car insurance and mechanics. They provide notary services and can help you register your car and get a license plate. Membership costs $39 per year for basic membership and an additional $28 for AAA Plus membership, a program that provides more services. Call **412-362-1491** if you have questions about joining AAA.

Public Transportation

Other than driving, there are several ways to travel in and around Pittsburgh. Depending on where you live and work, you might take a bus, train, taxi, walk, or even ride your bike.

Public transportation in Pittsburgh and Allegheny County is run by Port Authority Transit (PAT). They have many buses and a few trains that go throughout the city of Pittsburgh and the suburbs. Bus service within the city is good, especially during the weekdays. Service for the

Public Transportation Advantages

- Express trains and buses can sometimes take you where you want to go faster than by car, especially during rush hours (7:00–9:00 a.m. and 3:00–6:30 p.m.)

- It is difficult to find parking spaces in many areas of the city, such as downtown and Oakland. If you take the bus, you will not have to find a parking space.

- Public transportation is less expensive than paying for gasoline and parking every day.

- It is environmentally better for the city when people take buses and leave their cars at home.

suburbs is generally limited to providing transportation for people going to and from downtown. Service from one suburb to another is almost nonexistent, and you should be aware of this when making travel plans. For example, it is difficult to go from Monroeville to Penn Hills by bus. It is sometimes difficult to get bus service after 6:00 p.m. or on the weekend; in fact, many suburbs have little or no Sunday bus service.

It is helpful to visit the **PAT Service Center** to learn about public transportation. It is located at 534 Smithfield Street (downtown next to Mellon Square). At the service center you can get a free system map that shows all the bus and train lines. They also have free schedules for every bus. You can call them at **412-442-2000** to find out specific information about bus routes.

Service areas are divided into zones. A ride within zone 1 costs $1.25. A ride between zone 1 and zone 2 costs $1.60. You can buy weekly and monthly passes or a booklet of tickets that will reduce the cost of public transit. PAT bus #28X provides transportation to and from the airport. You may purchase a transfer for $.25. It may be used within three hours of its purchase.

Taxis

The best place to find taxis is downtown in front of the large hotels (The Hilton, Westin William Penn, The Ramada Plaza Suites, and Doubletree Hotels). You can also find them at the Greyhound bus and Amtrak train stations as well as at the airport. Taxis are especially convenient for travel at night when bus service is reduced. Unlike in New York City, you cannot expect to stop a taxi driving down the street. You can call for a taxi to pick you up and take you to your door.

When you call for a taxi, the service operator will ask for your name, where you are, and where you want to go. He or she will tell you when your taxi will arrive. It might come sooner than promised, but do not be surprised if you have to wait longer. If you know in advance where and when you want to go, call for a taxi to meet you at a specific time and place.

Pittsburgh taxi companies

Yellow Cab Company	412-665-8100
Peoples Cab Company	412-681-3131
Blue & White Taxi Company	412-421-2227

Food

Eating at Restaurants

If you go into any store where magazines and newspapers are sold, chances are that you will find a number of guides for "eating out" (that is, outside your home) in Pittsburgh. Local newspapers list addresses and descriptions of local restaurants, usually in Friday editions. *Pittsburgh Magazine*, too, carries a monthly restaurant guide, as do many other local publications.

After you have found some restaurants you would like to visit, you might want to review some general American restaurant etiquette, or rules, so you can enjoy your restaurant lunch or dinner with confidence.

- Many restaurants in Pittsburgh—particularly those of better quality—require you to make reservations, that is, to call the restaurant before you arrive in order to reserve a table for a certain time. Try to call at least two hours ahead, particularly on the weekend.

- As you drive up to an elegant restaurant, you might see a Valet Parking sign. This indicates that a parking attendant on the premises will, after you step out of the car and give him or her your car keys, park your car for you in the parking lot. This is a courtesy extended to you by the restaurant. It is customary to tip the attendant after you leave again to pick up your car.

- When you arrive inside the restaurant, you will usually see a large sign requesting you to "Please Wait to be Seated." Americans rarely, and only if it is indicated by a sign, walk into a restaurant and sit anywhere they wish. A seat will be found for you by a maître d', a host, a hostess, or waiter. You will never be seated with a table of strangers. It is not the custom in the United States for people who do not know each other to share a single table.

- In many restaurants, customers are not permitted to smoke. In those where it is allowed, sections are divided between smoking and non-smoking. Be sure that you are in the appropriate section before smoking.

- It is still considered mannerly for a man to pull out a chair for a woman—or for anyone significantly older—and to wait for his companion to be seated before he sits down.

- It is customary for people to order drinks and hors d'oeuvres before dinner. A first course might consist of a soup or salad. Salads are eaten before the main course. Ask the waiter for recommendations concerning the appetizers, or hors d'oeuvres. Today, business people rarely order alcohol before or during business lunches.

- Before the evening meal, particularly if it is a private occasion, you might wish to order a bottle of wine. You are probably familiar with the procedure for ordering from the wine steward, or *sommelier*. Americans are usually not extremely critical with the choice of wine. It is rare for a wine—or a dish—to be sent back to the kitchen, but if either is truly unacceptable, feel free to do so.

- Some table manners might be similar to those in your home country; Americans, for example, do not put their elbows on the table at any time during the restaurant visit. Instead, the left hand rests in the lap when not in use, and the right is occupied with the fork. Of course, both hands are needed when cutting somthing with a knife. Americans do not hold the knife and fork in their hands at all times, as do Europeans. Instead, they use the knife to cut single pieces of food before returning the hand momentarily to resting position. If you are unsure about how to do this, watch your American neighbors.

- It is also not customary to stack used dishes together. Instead, wait for the waiter to stack them and carry them away. It is also unusual, of course, for any attention to be paid to personal appearance at the table—do not apply lipstick, comb your hair, or visibly straighten your clothing. Do such tasks in the restroom. It is also not customary to point, shout, or snap your fingers when signalling the waiter during the meal. Instead, make eye contact and slightly raise one finger if you need something. If you cannot get the waiter's attention, say, "Excuse me," when he or she passes by.

- Americans often order coffee and dessert after the main course of the meal. The waiter will be happy to supply you with a list of dessert choices.

- At finer restaurants you can pay your bill at your table. This is a common practice that has the waiter/waitress process your check while you stay seated at your table. At other restaurants customers usually pay at the cash register.

- Many Pittsburgh restaurants accept credit cards. Please inquire about this policy before you have been seated for your meal. After you have finished you will want to leave the waiter a tip. (See the "Tipping" sidebar on page 44.)

- Americans frequently take home uneaten portions of their meals by requesting the waiter/waitress to bring them a "doggie bag." This practice is very common and is not considered to be taboo.

These hints will ensure you many pleasant visits to Pittsburgh's restaurants. Bon Appetit!

Eating at Home

Most Americans buy food in supermarkets, large stores with a selection of food including fresh fruit, vegetables, meat, and canned foods. You can also buy other household items such as soap, pet food, and cooking utensils in a supermarket. You might also be able to rent videos, buy popular books and magazines, and go to a bank in the supermarket. Four large supermarkets in the Pittsburgh area are Giant Eagle, Foodland, Shop N' Save, and Food Gallery.

Supermarkets advertise special prices in local newspapers, such as the *Pittsburgh Post-Gazette* or the *Pittsburgh Tribune-Review*. You can save money on some food items if you use coupons. A coupon is a small piece of paper advertising a lower price for a particular food item. Cut the coupon out of the newspaper and give it to the cashier when you pay for your food. Some supermarkets issue free customer cards known as "frequent buyer cards" that they use to give discounts on advertised items.

Because they are convenient, most people buy their food in supermarkets. However, there are other stores where you can find specialty food items. Specialty foods include imported foods and organic foods, which is food grown or produced without using chemicals. Specialty food stores often have fresher vegetables, fruits, meat, and fish than supermarkets, often at higher prices than in supermarkets.

The Strip District is Pittsburgh's daily food market. It is famous for its fresh fruit, vegetables, meat, fish, and cheese stores. This is the best place in Pittsburgh to find a good selection of foods from other countries. It is located on Smallman Street and Penn Avenue between 11th and 31st Streets near the downtown area. Many stores in the Strip open early in the morning, around 7:00 a.m. and close around 3:00 or 4:00 p.m

Some Pittsburgh specialty food stores

Alex's International Foods: 2020 Smallman Street, Strip District, 412-232-0960. Russian and East European Foods.

East End Food Co-op: 7516 Meade Street, Point Breeze, 412-242-3598. An excellent store for organic vegetables, fruits, and processed natural foods. They have a large selection of herbs, spices, flour, and whole grains.

Goldenseal: 2731 Murray Avenue, Squirrel Hill, 412-422-7455. Herbs and natural foods.

Labad's: 1727 Penn Avenue, Strip District, 412-261-0419. Middle Eastern Foods.

La Charcuterie: 5863 Ellsworth Avenue, Shadyside, 412-661-6642. Imported foods from Europe including cheeses, coffees, chocolate, and bread.

Kohli Indian Imports: 319 South Craig Street, Oakland, 412-621-1800. Foods from Asia including Bismati rice. Also, Indian videos and music.

Kim Do Oriental Grocery: 1808 Penn Avenue, Strip District, 412-338-6588. Asian food.

Murray Avenue Kosher: 1916 Murray Avenue, Squirrel Hill, 412-421-4450. Grocery with a selection of kosher meats.

McGinnis Sisters Special Food Stores: 4311 Northern Pike, Monroeville, 412-858-7000/3825 SawMill Run Blvd., 412-882-6400. Grocery specializing in fresh fish, meat, and some imported foods.

Penns Woods Organics Market: 2316 Penn Avenue, Strip District, 412-765-1964. Organic foods and vegetables.

Pennsylvania Macaroni Company: 2012 Penn Avenue, Strip District, 412-471-8330. Cheese, pasta, and imported foods.

Salem & Hnesh Halal Meats Inc.: 340 South Bouquet Street, Oakland, 412-621-4354. Mid-Eastern foods and catering.

Tokyo Japanese Food Store: 5853 Ellsworth Avenue, Shadyside, 412-661-3777. Food imported from Japan.

Wholey's: 1711 Penn Avenue, Strip District, 412-391-3737. Fresh seafood and meats.

Farmers' Markets

A good place to find fresh vegetables is at one of the weekly farmers' markets in the city. The markets are open from May 12 to late November from 4 to 8 p.m.

Cookware

You can buy cookware, also called housewares—cooking equipment such as pots, pans, knives, plates—at all department stores, culinary stores in malls, and at specialty cookware stores throughout the city.

Farmers' Markets

Highland Park: Mondays and Thursdays in the lower parking lot of the Pittsburgh Zoo at Butler and Baker Street.

South Side: Tuesdays at South 18th Street and Sydney Street.

Carrick: Wednesdays next to the Carrick Shopping Center.

North Side: Fridays in West Park next to Allegheny Center Mall.

Shopping

Finding almost everything you need—and many things you do not need—is easy in the United States. For some Americans, shopping is a major free-time activity. Stores advertise aggressively and constantly in the newspapers, on radio, on TV, in the Internet, by mail, and on billboards. If you look hard, you might be able to find many of the same products you used in your home country.

As a newcomer, you might need to get some things to help you establish yourself and your home. You can look up general categories, such as "Furniture" and "Hardware" in the Yellow Pages telephone book for most stores and services in the Pittsburgh area. The Yellow Pages not only provides a comprehensive selection of all items you might wish to buy, it also offers in these same sections the names of shops where you can get these items repaired.

Clothing

Although much of the United States is shifting toward more casual office attire, Pittsburgh still leans more toward conservative dress. Pittsburgh professionals favor a wardrobe full of classic suits and separates. If you are male, an English-cut suit, solid-colored shirt, and necktie are standard apparel for most of the work week. For women, suit jackets with matching knee-length skirts or pants, high-heeled shoes, and restrained jewelry are the norm. Working Pittsburghers appreciate solid dark colors and natural materials; most of them are more concerned with looking competent than with wearing the latest fashions.

Many workplaces over the past several years have promoted the concept of casual Fridays, or less conservative dress to help boost employee morale. This new policy has caused some confusion about appropriate attire. If your company has instituted such a policy and you are not sure what to wear, ask your personnel director, supervisor, or colleagues. If, after asking, you are still not sure, it is better to err on the side of formality—blue jeans and tee shirts are much too casual for most workplaces, even on casual Friday!

If you are going out to dinner or to a club after work, office attire is usually appropriate. Ask your co-workers or friends for suggestions about what to wear to specific places. If you are attending the opera, ballet, or other evening event, formal dress is usually required, although people sometimes dress less formally. This is also true for any private invitation calling for "black tie" or "white tie." If guests are not sure what to wear, they often call to ask the host or hostess for advice.

You can get appropriate clothes for any occasion at department stores, such as Kaufmann's, Lazarus, J.C. Penney, Sears, and Saks Fifth Avenue. Many people shop in malls—large indoor shopping centers—where you can find department stores as well as smaller boutique-style shops. Most salespeople will be helpful in advising you about which items of clothing to wear for specific occasions.

Shadyside, Squirrel Hill, One Oxford Center, Station Square, and The Galleria have many smaller boutiques and specialty stores.

Discount stores, such as Sym's, T.J. Maxx, Marshall's, and Burlington Coat Factory, charge lower prices, and the clothes they sell might be from a prior season. You can find a variety of department stores downtown and in neighborhood business districts.

Many people enjoy shopping at "outlet" malls, such as Grove City and Somerset, where shops often offer designer clothing at discounted prices. Grove City, one of the largest outlet malls in the country, is an hour's drive from Pittsburgh.

If you do not find what you are looking for in any of these places, you might want to investigate the world of mail-order catalogues. Many mail-order companies advertise in magazines, and many of them also offer shopping via sites on the World Wide Web.

Hair Care

The Yellow Pages lists many hair care salons under the heading "Beauty Salons." Many malls and department stores have salons. You can also often get a perfectly good haircut at a lower priced chain salon or barber shop.

Furniture

You can find furniture at large furniture stores, such as IKEA, Weisshouse, Levin Furniture Company, Katilius, Houseworks, Today's Home, Wickes, among many others. Most major department stores have furniture departments. Many of these stores advertise frequent sales. There are also many smaller stores located in malls, neighborhoods, and shopping centers. Check the Yellow Pages to find the addresses for stores convenient to you.

Auction houses, a large group of antique shops in Wexford, a similarly large group in Canonsburg and the South Hills, and the monthly summer antique fair in Hanna's Town represent several possibilities for successful antique hunting. You will be pleasantly surprised with the prices of Pittsburgh's collectibles, particularly if you are moving here from another large city. If you have a chance, drive to one of neighboring Ohio's many flea markets in the spring. These open-air events are also advertised in Pittsburgh newspapers.

Decorators

Many full-service furniture stores can tell you where to turn when choosing a decorator. Check the Yellow Pages under "Interior Decorators" for other possibilities.

Art

Pittsburgh is a city for art lovers. If you are looking to buy fine art, visit the Pittsburgh Center for the Arts or one of the many other gallery spaces listed in the Yellow Pages under "Art Galleries, Dealers & Consultants."

Jewelry

Pittsburgh has many good jewelry stores. The Clark Building in downtown Pittsburgh has many jewelry stores located within it. The city is also full of smaller neighborhood shops that specialize in personal service. Check local newspapers and *Pittsburgh Magazine* for advertisements.

Cookware

As mentioned previously, most department stores sell cooking equipment such as pots, pans, knives, plates. Also try Wholey's, Lechter's, IKEA, and The Home Place, among others.

Fabrics

Discount Decorator Fabrics and The Textile Studio carry excellent selections of reasonably priced fabrics for home decorating. For sewing clothing, national chains of fabrics and craft stores, such as Jo-Anne Fabrics & Crafts and Minnesota Fabrics, have frequent sales. For other choices, check the Yellow Pages under "Fabric Shops."

Florists

Check the Yellow Pages for listings of full-scale floral shops. Some grocery stores sell pre-made bouquets, and street vendors often have cut flowers for sale as well.

Hardware

You can buy tools, garden supplies, paint, and building materials at a hardware store. Local hardware stores, such as Rolliers in Mt. Lebanon, are located in almost every business district. Chain stores, such as Home Depot, Lowe's, and Hechinger are usually in major shopping areas.

Books, Magazines, and Newspapers

Large chain bookstores, such as Borders and Barnes & Noble, and many excellent independent bookstores in the area offer books, music, children's literature, and magazines. Several good used booksellers can be found on Carson Street in the South Side and around Craig Street in Oakland. Most of these bookstores have children's books, too. The University Book Center at the University of Pittsburgh has some foreign language news magazines.

Rugs

Check the "Carpet & Rug Dealers" listings in the Yellow Pages for area stores. Many large department stores also have carpet and rug departments.

Toys

You can find toys for children at large chain stores and in many smaller stores downtown and in Squirrel Hill. Discount department stores also sell toys.

Electronics and Computers

You can buy radios, CD players, TVs, telephones, microwave ovens, and computers at department stores and large electronic stores. Look in the Yellow Pages under "Stereophonic & High Fidelity Equipment," "Television," "Appliances," and "Computers."

Used Items

The quality of used clothes, cookware, furniture, and books at second hand stores and thrift shops varies widely. You can sometimes find incredible bargains—if you have the patience. Resale establishments can be found by checking the Yellow Pages under "Thrift Shops." Some of the more well known include Goodwill, Salvation Army Thrift Shops, Red and White Thrift Store, and the St. Vincent De Paul Society.

In the spring and summer, many people advertise "garage sales" or "yard sales," where they sell unneeded household goods from their homes. These are the least expensive places to get what you need. Check the classified ad section of your Sunday newspaper for garage sales in and around Pittsburgh.

Shopping "Rules" in the United States

Many stores advertise sales and special offers in newspapers and on TV. Waiting for an item to go on sale is a good way to save some money when shopping.

You can pay for items by cash, credit card, or check. If you pay by check, a cashier will likely ask for identification and your telephone number. Most shoppers find it more convenient to pay using cash or a credit card such as Visa or MasterCard.

If you want to return something you have bought, you must return the item with its original sales receipt. Stores have different return policies. Many will give you your money back, others will give you store credit. In all cases, the item must be clean and not have been damaged by you.

In most cases, you cannot bargain. The price on the price tag is the price of an item. Americans only bargain in certain situations: when buying a house, a car, items at garage and house sales, and items advertised in newspaper classified advertisements. Americans save money by watching and waiting for sales and special deals at stores, or by shopping at discount stores.

Shopping & Outlet Malls

SHOPPING MALLS

South Suburbs:

The Galleria - 1500 Washington Road, Mt. Lebanon
Century III Mall - 3075 Clairton Road, West Mifflin
South Hills Village - Fort Couch Road and Route 19, Upper St. Clair

North Suburbs:

Cranberry Mall - 20-111 Route 19, Freedom Road, Mars
Ross Park Mall - 1000 Ross Park Mall Drive
(off McKnight Road), North Hills
North Hills Village - 4801 McKnight Road, North Hills
Northway Mall - 8000 McKnight Road, North Hills
Waterworks Mall - 925 Freeport Road, Fox Chapel

East Suburbs:

Miracle Mile Shopping Center- 4055 Monroeville Boulevard, Monroeville
Monroeville Mall - Business Route 22, Monroeville

West Suburbs:

Airmall - Pittsburgh International Airport
Robinson Town Center - 300 Park Manor Drive, Robinson Township
Parkway Center Mall - 1165 McKinney Lane, Greentree

OUTLET MALLS

Northwest:

Grove City Factory Shops - Off I-79 at Exit 31, Grove City

Southeast:

Horizon Outlet Center - Off Pennsylvania Turnpike at Exit 10, Somerset

10 Religion

Many religious communities are active in the United States. The Pittsburgh area is unique in that there are large, stable, and active Jewish, Muslim, and Hindu communities as well as Greek and Russian Orthodox, Roman Catholic, and Protestant communities. Not only do these groups maintain places of worship— many churches with roots in Western and Eastern Europe, temples, mosques, and synagogues—but religious groups in Pittsburgh also provide social opportunities, support, and points of contact for people from other countries.

People from all over the world have been coming to Pittsburgh for two centuries and have established places of worship throughout the city. Numerous synagogues can be found in the Squirrel Hill neighborhood. Pittsburgh's eastern suburbs are the home of a significant Indian Hindu population. Among several Hindu temples, are the Sri Venkateswara Temple in Penn Hills and the Hindu Jain Temple.

You can find the most complete list of places of worship (churches, temples, and mosques) in the Yellow Pages telephone book under "Churches." Non-Christian religions are listed here as well. For example, you can find a list of mosques in the Pittsburgh area under "Churches—Mosques." Jewish synagogues are listed separately under "Synagogues." Because America is a diverse country, all religious holidays cannot be listed

Religious Organizations and Associations

Catholic Diocese
111 Blvd. of the Allies
Pittsburgh, PA 15222
412-456-3000

Greek Orthodox Diocese
5201 Ellsworth Avenue
Pittsburgh, PA 15232
412-621-5529

United Jewish Federation of Greater Pittsburgh
234 McKee Place
Pittsburgh, PA 15213
412-681-8000

Islamic Center
4100 Bigelow Boulevard
Pittsburgh, PA 15213
412-682-5555

Sri Venkateswara
(S.V. Temple)
South McCully Drive
Pittsburgh, PA 15235
412-373-3380

Hindu Jain Temple
615 Illini Drive
Pittsburgh, PA 15146
412-325-2073

in this book. For information about important religious holidays such as Ramadan, please call the appropriate religious institutions listed in the Yellow Pages.

Education/Children

The vast majority of American children attend public schools. Public schools are tax supported and free to those who attend them. They include kindergarten through grade 12. After the 12th grade, many students go directly on to a higher level of education: college, junior college, or a trade school. In general, Americans must pay their own tuition for higher education.

School	Grades
Kindergarten	
Elementary school	1–6
Junior high school	
or Middle school	7–8
Senior high school	9–12

Class name	Grade
Freshman	9
Sophomore	10
Junior	11
Senior	12

Philosophy of U.S. Schools

There is no central, national administration in charge of U.S. public schools. Pennsylvania has its own guidelines. Each city, town, or community has a school district that is responsible for building, running, and supporting its own schools. They develop their own curricula, and have their own directors and budgets. In general, they all teach basic academic and learning skills: math, reading, writing, U.S. and world history, science, and some foreign languages, usually Spanish, French, German and sometimes Latin, Japanese, and Russian. Some schools start teaching languages at a young age and others start when children are older. It is not surprising that when many American families move, they choose their new locations according to the quality of the schools in that district.

Public education from kindergarten through 12th grade is intended for every child. Schools in the United States must meet the needs of every child, regardless of ability. The goal of education is to develop every child to the best of his or her capabilities, however great or small these might be. Another objective is to give each child a sense of civic and community consciousness.

American Teaching Style

American teaching styles tend to be informal compared to teaching styles found in other countries. Schools sometimes encourage innovative techniques. There is less emphasis on learning facts in the classroom and more emphasis on problem solving.

Students are taught to think for themselves, to explore, and to develop creative and intellectual abilities. There is growing emphasis on teaching computer skills.

Standards and Evaluation

Most schools evaluate grades using a letter system: A, B, C, D, F. A is the highest grade and F the lowest. Generally, good students earn As and Bs, average students receive Cs, poor student work receives a D or F grade. Schools will sometimes give precise grades by adding a "+" or "-" to the letters. Teachers give grades to students based on tests, quizzes (brief, unannounced tests), projects, writing assignments, and class participation. Schools send children's grades to parents several times a year, at the end of a grading period, on a report card. A report card will list each subject your child has been studying in school next to a letter grade. A report card might also include written comments from your child's teacher about how well he or she is doing in school. Parents should be sure to see what information appears in their child's records.

English as a Second Language (ESL)

Children are great language learners and adapt quickly to new language environments. Almost all schools in Western Pennsylvania teach in English. As a result your child might need time and help adjusting to learning subjects such as reading and social sciences in English.

Pennsylvania schools are required to accommodate students who do not speak English as their native language. Pennsylvania law says that "every school district shall provide a program for each student whose dominant language is not English for the purpose of facilitating the student's achievement of English proficiency. Programs under this section shall include appropriate bilingual-bicultural or English as a second language instruction." (Title 22, Chapter 5, Section 5.216 Pennsylvania School Code.)

The state's law is not specific about how and to what extent schools must teach these students. School districts in Western Pennsylvania provide specialized teaching and extra instruction in a variety of ways. Pittsburgh public schools, for example, have their own special teachers and programs for teaching English as a second language (ESL). Other school districts, however, might have to make special arrangements or contact the Allegheny Intermediate Unit as a resource to set up special teaching.

It is important that the parents of children who do not speak English as their native language take an active role in their child's education. Although some schools might not have much experience with foreign students, they will be better able to help your child if they have a good understanding of your child's level of English.

After you have found a place to live and locate the school where your child will study, contact that school's administration directly and set up an appointment with the school's principal or representative. The earlier schools know about your child, the better. They will have more time to locate the right teachers. Provide as much information about your child's past schooling as possible.

Schools in the United States are open to parents and encourage them to actively participate in educating their children. Feel free to talk to your child's teacher as well as to the principal and counselors at his or her school.

Some local groups have organized educational programs that supplement U.S. public education. These programs take place on weekends and evenings during the school year. Their purpose is to keep students learning at the same pace as students in their home country. Programs are privately organized and require fees. An example of this is the Pittsburgh Japanese School (412-422-4428).

English Classes

Several schools, agencies, and firms offer language classes in the Pittsburgh area. You can take classes in a variety of settings, from one-on-one ESL classes to group classes with fellow students from around the world. Most programs charge by the number of hours for which a student is enrolled. Some programs are designed for lower income foreign newcomers. Others are designed for professionals who need to improve their English skills for scientific and business communication. The following lists some Pittsburgh ESL institutions. When you call university-affiliated offices for information about their ESL programs, they might refer you to other university offices for admission information.

University Programs

The English Language Institute at the University of Pittsburgh offers ESL classes to adults at low and high intermediate to advanced levels (there are no beginner classes). The English Language Institute also offers an informal Spouse's Course between May and August of ever year. You can call **412-624-9174** to register for the Spouse's Course. Classes are offered each semester.

Admissions Officer
English Language Institute
Department of Linguistics
2816 Cathedral of Learning
University of Pittsburgh
Pittsburgh, PA 15260
412-624-5901
E-mail: elipitt@pitt.edu

Duquesne University's ESL Program offers English classes to adults preparing for university studies as well as those who just want to study English. Group classes are offered each semester.

English as a Second Language Office
304 Des Places Language Center
Duquesne University
Pittsburgh, PA 15282-1230
412-396-5091

Point Park College has an ESL program for students and other adults from beginners to advanced. Group classes are offered each semester.

Office of International Admissions (ESL Office)
Point Park College
201 Wood Street
Pittsburgh, PA 15222-1984
412-392-3925

Community College of Allegheny County offers classes at several locations throughout Allegheny County. Group classes are offered each semester.

Community College of Allegheny County
800 Allegheny Avenue
Pittsburgh, PA 15233-1895
412-237-2511

Personalized Programs

Echo International (formerly known as The Language Center, Inc.) in downtown Pittsburgh provides complete and personalized English as a Second Language (ESL) instruction for every level of ability. Teachers are university graduates with a deep understanding and appreciation for the languages and cultural information with which they work. In addition to ESL, this company offers cross-cultural training and translation services. Classes are offered by arrangement to accommodate each student's individual needs.

Echo International
313 Sixth Avenue, Fourth Floor
Pittsburgh, PA 15222
412-261-1101

Other ESL programs offered by private firms can be found in the Yellow Pages under "Language Schools."

Agency Programs

Connelley Technical Institute and Adult Education Center offers group ESL classes by arrangement.

Connelley Technical Institute
1501 Bedford Avenue
Pittsburgh, PA 15219-3695
Room 311
412-338-3710

ACCESL (Allegheny County Center for ESL) also offers ESL classes by appointment. (Free or low cost)

ACCESL
1401 Forbes Avenue
Pittsburgh, PA 15219
412-281-4494

Adult Education

Adults can take classes at local universities and colleges even if they are not interested in receiving academic or professional degrees. These classes for adults have several names: informal classes, continuing education classes, or lifelong learning classes.

Many continuing education classes are the same as classes taken by regular university students. Classes are designed to meet the particular interests of adults who already have a university degree, but who are still interested in learning. Most adults taking continuing education classes want to pursue their own academic interests or improve professional skills. Continuing education classes also provide an opportunity to meet other people in the Pittsburgh area. The International Women's Association of Pittsburgh (412-441-8102), for example, offers informal conversation groups.

Continuing education classes often meet when busy and working adults can attend—during the weekends and in the evenings. For some programs, you do not need to have a university degree. You can contact local universities and colleges to ask about classes, schedules, costs, and requirements.

Community College of Allegheny County (CCAC) has a unique mission to meet the educational needs and interests of the general public in Allegheny County. Classes are inexpensive and you can take classes with or without a university degree. CCAC offers a diverse selection of academic, general interest, and practical classes such as cooking.

Community College of Allegheny County
Lifelong Learning
Allegheny Campus
808 Ridge Avenue
Pittsburgh, PA 15212
412-325-6643

Duquesne University
Division of Continuing Education
Duquesne University
212 Rockwell Hall
Pittsburgh, PA 15282-0102
412-396-5034

University of Pittsburgh
College of General Studies
Pitt's Informal Program
Room 407 Cathedral of Learning
Pittsburgh, PA 15260
412-648-2560

Carlow College
Continuing Education
3333 Fifth Avenue
Pittsburgh, PA 15213
412-578-6092

In addition to classes at local colleges and universities, several organizations offer opportunities for adults to pursue special interests.

Point Park College offers arts classes for adults in theater, dance, and music. Call 412-392-3456 for information about dance and music classes. Call 412-621-3948 for information about theater and musical theater classes.

Pittsburgh Center for the Arts offers arts classes for adults in 20 artistic areas. Call 412-361-0455.

The Carnegie Museums of Pittsburgh offer writing, natural history, art history, painting, and sculpture classes as well as lectures, and travel opportunities to adults. Call 412-622-3288.

Child Care

Being a parent with young children in the United States might be different from being a parent in your home country. A busy American lifestyle and job requirements can conflict with the traditional roles of parents. If your child is not old enough to go to school and you are working, you might find it difficult to spend large amounts of time at home with your child.

American mothers and fathers sometimes exchange parenting roles and share child care responsibilities. In order to raise their children and hold full or part-time jobs, parents often pay for some kind of child care services. A variety of child care arrangements are available in the Pittsburgh area.

There are a number of important things to understand about child care services in general. There are several types of child care available: child care centers, group care, and family care. Some are nonprofit centers and others are for profit. Although the State of Pennsylvania does license and register different types of child care services, the quality of child care services does vary. Some services are excellent, some services are not.

In some cases, you will find that good child care is expensive. However, price does not always correspond to quality. It is important that parents take an active and long-term interest in where their child spends his or her day. It is a good idea to visit several places, talk with child caregivers (the teachers), and administrators before enrolling your child at a child care service. Good care is available, but you must sometimes look for it.

Child Care Centers

Child care centers (also known as day care) are licensed by the State of Pennsylvania. At a child care center, your child spends the day (or part of the day) with other children in the same age group. Children are watched over by a qualified adult staff of caregivers. Children play, participate in learning and development activities appropriate for their age group, and are fed lunch and snacks. Day care center programs and hours vary. A child care center might be able to accommodate your work schedule.

Group Care

Group care services are registered (not licensed) by the state. Group care centers are less formally administered than child care centers. The number of children they can care for is limited by the state.

Family Care

Family care services are also registered by the state. They can be run in private homes but must care for six or fewer children. Some family care is legally unregistered, that is, they care for four or fewer children.

There is such a thing as unofficial child care also known as "underground child care" because it is illegal. Unofficial child care services are neither registered nor licensed by the state. They are unofficial because they do not comply with state regulations. Avoid unofficial child care.

When considering a child care service (a day care center, group care center, or family care service) there are several things you should look for:

- How many teachers are there for each child? Generally, infants (babies) should be cared for in small groups because they require more attention. Older children, toddlers, and preschool-aged children can be cared for in larger groups.

- Will your child spend his or her day with the same children every day? It is important that children be with the same group of children and have the same caregivers over a long period of time. It is important that children not be put in an unstable environment because they must have time to form stable relationships.

- How experienced are the staff? Have they been specially trained to care for children in a day care setting? Is there a lot of caregiver turnover? Does the service have to keep hiring new caregivers to replace those who have left?

- What are the day care facilities like? Are they clean? Are there appropriate toys and other play and learning materials? Do children spend time outside?

- What is the children's daily schedule? Is it varied? Does it include naps, meals, and activities? How much TV, if any, are the children allowed to watch? If the children do watch TV, is it as part of a larger activity or just to keep the children occupied?

- Does the service encourage parents to visit at any time and without notice? Good services allow parents to visit occasionally to see what their children are doing at the center.

YWCA of Greater Pittsburgh Childcare Partnerships has a referral service and child care information service. You can call Childcare Partnerships with questions about how to find quality child care. Call them at 412-261-CARE (2273).

The National Association for the Education of Young Children (NAEYC) can send you a brochure with guidelines to help you evaluate child care programs. Ask for *Finding the Best Care for Your Infant or Toddler* (#518). You can contact NAEYC at 1-800-424-2460.

You can find the names of child care services in the Pittsburgh area in the Yellow Pages telephone book under "Child Day Care."

Baby-sitters

Parents occasionally hire someone—a baby-sitter—to watch their children when they are away for an evening or afternoon. Often, baby-sitters are teenagers who have time after school or on weekends and want to earn extra money. Parents of young children often know several baby-sitters they can trust to watch and take care of their children. Some baby-sitters are the teenage children of friends and neighbors. Others are trusted adults who have the time to watch children. Hiring a baby sitter is an informal arrangement between you and the baby-sitter. You pay a baby-sitter between $5 and $10 per hour. Ask colleagues, neighbors, and friends to recommend a good baby-sitter for you.

Activities for Children

A large number of organizations offer activity programs for children in Pittsburgh and the suburbs. Children can participate in sports, arts, special education, and social programs. Programs take place after school, on the weekend, and during the summer for children of all ages.

Having your children participate in these organizations is a great way for them to meet others their age and learn new skills. It is also an opportunity for parents to meet other adults whose children are part of these activities.

This is a partial listing of the opportunities available for children, but this list will get you started. Many organizations advertise programs in local newspapers, libraries, community centers, and at schools. Feel free to contact these and other organizations. They can send you information about program content, schedules, age groups, locations, and costs.

Most programs require parents to pay at least a small fee for their children to participate. Some provide financial aid—a reduced fee or money to help pay for participation costs. Financial aid helps children from lower income families participate. You might wish to ask about financial aid when you call.

Pittsburgh Center for the Arts has a Summer Arts Camp, a series of week-long camps where children actively learn about music, dance, painting, sculpture, drama, and writing.

Pittsburgh Center for the Arts
1047 Shady Avenue
Pittsburgh, PA 15232
412-361-0455

Western Pennsylvania Boys and Girls Clubs is one of the largest organizations in the area and has a large variety of activities and programs for children during the year. Programs include, sports, social, special education, and summer camps.

Western Pennsylvania Boys and Girls Clubs
4412 Butler Street
Pittsburgh, PA 15201
412-682-3031

YMCA of Pittsburgh (Young Men's Christian Association) is one of the largest organizations providing special programs for children (and adults). Programs include summer camps, sports programs, arts, special education, and social services. The YMCA has programs for boys and girls, men and women. Programs are open to persons of all religions. Consult the White Pages telephone book for the YMCA closest to your home.

YWCA of Pittsburgh (Young Women's Christian Association) has programs for women and children including sports, health, and support groups at locations throughout the city. You can call their main offices for information. Programs are open to persons of all religions.

YWCA of Pittsburgh
305 Wood Street
Pittsburgh, PA 15222
412-391-5100

The Carnegie Museum of Art and the **Carnegie Museum of Natural History** offer educational programs and classes in art (sculpture, painting, and crafts) and science for children.

Carnegie Museum of Art and Carnegie Museum of Natural History
4400 Forbes Avenue
Pittsburgh, PA 15213-4080
412-622-3288

12 Medicine

Medical care in the Pittsburgh area is of high quality. You can find doctors, dentists, optometrists and medical specialists throughout the Pittsburgh area. There are hospitals, clinics, and doctors' offices located in the city and the suburbs.

There is no centralized medical care system in the United States or comprehensive medical insurance coverage. People who have medical insurance receive it as a benefit through their employer or buy it on their own from an insurance provider. The trend is toward creating large systems that provide coordinated medical care and insurance coverage. You might discover that finding the kind of doctor you need is fairly easy, finding and understanding coverage to pay for medical services is more complicated. The biggest criticism of health care in the United States is that it is expensive.

The most helpful place to find out about medical care for you and your family is with your employer or at the school you attend. Employees often qualify for group coverage through the company for which they work. University students can get affordable health coverage through their universities.

Medical Care

You can find a doctor, dentist, optometrist, or specialist in several places. In addition to the sources listed below, you can ask friends and colleagues to recommend a good doctor, dentist, or optometrist.

Look in the Yellow Pages to find the names of doctors and specialists under "Physicians," "Dentists," and "Optical—Optometrists." You can find the names of area hospitals under "Hospitals."

Physician Referral Numbers of Major Pittsburgh Hospitals

Allegheny General Hospital
412-359-3027

Children's Hospital of Pittsburgh
412-692-7337

Magee-Women's Hospital
412-647-4747

Mercy Hospital
412-232-5660

St. Francis Hospital
800-537-9069

University of Pittsburgh Medical Center (UPMC)
412-647-8762

The Western Pennsylvania Hospital
412-362-8677

Many hospitals have a telephone referral service. When you call a referral service, a hospital representative will tell you the names of the kinds of doctors who work at the hospital. When you call a doctor referral service, they will tell you about doctors who speak your native language (if any), translating services, doctors for children, gynecologists, and other specialists.

Many of Pittsburgh's hospitals have experience treating patients from other countries.

Major Western Pennsylvania health insurance companies

Highmark Blue Cross/ Blue Shield
Fifth Avenue Place
120 Fifth Avenue,
Suite 1124
Pittsburgh, PA 15222
1-800-253-5200

Aetna U.S. Healthcare
2 Marquis Plaza,
Suite 300
5313 Campbells Run Rd.
Pittsburgh, PA 15205
1-800-323-9930

HealthAmerica of Pittsburgh
Five Gateway Center
Pittsburgh, PA 15222
412-553-7300

Medical Insurance

As soon as you arrive, you should begin to find out about medical coverage for you and your family. Paying for doctor's visits, especially emergency services and major medical care, is extremely expensive without insurance that pays some or all of your medical bills. Many Americans (although not all) have some kind of medical insurance coverage. Some have individual or family medical coverage through their employer. Others pay for individual or family coverage by themselves.

There are many kinds of medical insurance available. Costs, terms of coverage, and bill payment methods vary greatly. Whether or not you have insurance coverage through your job or school or need to find it by yourself, you should be sure to understand certain things.

Costs

You can pay for insurance coverage monthly, quarterly, or yearly depending on the company. Paying for health insurance is expensive but paying hospital bills yourself is much more expensive. A visit to a doctor's office for a routine checkup costs about $50. The cost of delivering a baby in a hospital, with no complications, can cost as much as $7,000. Doctor and hospital costs vary.

Many insurance companies require you to pay part of a bill for medical services. Some insurance companies might pay a percentage of a medical bill and require you to pay a *co-payment*—a fixed amount for each service. Other insurance companies

---

require you to pay a *deductible*—a fixed amount of money before they pay for the rest of the bill. Still other insurance companies require you to pay for medical services yourself and apply to them for reimbursement. Others pay the medical service provider, such as a hospital or doctor, directly.

Terms of Coverage

You should know what medical services your insurance company will and will not pay for. They should provide you with a brochure and information that describes how they pay for medical services and what you should do.

Questions to ask about medical coverage

- Will they pay for a baby's delivery as well as prenatal and postnatal care?

- Will they pay for routine care such as a yearly examination by a doctor?

- Do you have to get a referral from or permission from the insurance company or a doctor before you visit a medical specialist?

- Can you visit a doctor near your home or do you have to travel to an office in a faraway location?

- How will your insurance cover you when you travel in the United States or to another country?

- What should you do in an emergency? Is there a special phone number you have to call for emergency medical advice? What emergency medical service items are covered?

13 Exploring

During your stay in Pittsburgh, there are some places you simply must visit. Every longtime resident in Pittsburgh and Western Pennsylvania knows about these museums, amusement parks, and special places—they show off what is best about the city and its surrounding areas. These are excellent places to go as a family during weekends. Of course, there are too many interesting places in the area to list here completely, but here is a list (offered in part by the Greater Pittsburgh Museum Council) concerning attractions in Pittsburgh and Western Pennsylvania:

Performing Arts

Pittsburgh has a very rich cultural tradition.   Below are listed a few of the many performing arts organizations in the community. There are numerous other performing groups that may also be of interest to you. There is a listing of arts organizations in the Yellow Pages under "Arts Organizations & Information." Each Friday, the *Pittsburgh Post-Gazette* and *Pittsburgh Tribune-Review* list weekend performances. The newspapers also list performers at clubs as well as movies and upcoming concerts of all types of music. *Pittsburgh Magazine, InPittsburgh* and the *City Paper* also list performances in Pittsburgh.   In the summer, the newspapers have listings of many free concerts in the area at places such as Point State Park, Hartwood Acres, Mellon Park and the Carnegie Museums of Pittsburgh.

Music

Pittsburgh Symphony Orchestra
Heinz Hall for the Performing Arts
600 Penn Avenue
Pittsburgh, PA 15222
412-392-4900
The world renowned Pittsburgh Symphony Orchestra under the musical direction of Mariss Jansons performs at Heinz Hall for the Performing Arts in downtown Pittsburgh. The Symphony also offers a series of popular musical performances.

Pittsburgh Chamber Music Society

P.O. Box 81066

Pittsburgh, PA 15217

412-624-4129

The Pittsburgh Chamber Music Society brings world-class chamber music groups to the Carnegie Music Hall in Oakland for a series of Monday evening concerts.

Renaissance & Baroque Society of Pittsburgh

303 S. Craig Street

Pittsburgh, PA 15213

412-682-7262

Performances by musicians using authentic period instruments are featured in this group's series of concerts, held in Synod Hall in Oakland.

River City Brass Band

P.O. Box 6436

Pittsburgh, PA 15212

412-322-7222

The River City Brass Band produces an annual concert series of musical programs throughout the region. The concerts in Pittsburgh are performed at the Carnegie Music Hall.

Y Music Society

5738 Forbes Avenue

Pittsburgh, PA 15217

412-521-8011

The Y Music Society of the Jewish Community Center offers all of Pittsburgh a series of the world's leading musical talent in the intimate setting of a recital hall. The performances are presented at the Carnegie Music Hall in Oakland.

Opera

Pittsburgh Opera
717 Penn Avenue, 8th Floor
Pittsburgh, PA 15222
412-456-6666
The Pittsburgh Opera offers a series of operas, often featuring internationally known performers. The operas are performed at the Benedum Center .

Musical Theater

Civic Light Opera
719 Liberty Avenue
Pittsburgh, PA 15222
412-281-3973
Each summer, the Civic Light Opera presents a series of Broadway musicals at the Benedum Center.

MasterCard Broadway Series Pittsburgh
719 Liberty Avenue
Pittsburgh, PA 15222
412-471-6930
The MasterCard Pittsburgh Broadway Series is a presentation of the Pittsburgh Symphony Society, The Pittsburgh Cultural Trust and PACE Theatrical Group, Inc. Performances are presented at the Benedum Center, Heinz Hall and the Byham Theater.

Ballet

Pittsburgh Ballet Theatre
2900 Liberty Avenue
Pittsburgh, PA 15201
412-281-0360
One of the top seven ballet companies in the United States, the Pittsburgh Ballet Theatre performs at the Benedum Center.

Modern Dance

Pittsburgh Dance Council
719 Liberty Avenue
Pittsburgh, PA 15222
412-355-0330
The Pittsburgh Dance Council is the premiere presenter of contemporary dance companies from around the world. Performances take place at the Benedum Center and the Byham Theater.

Theater

City Theatre Company
557 South 13th Street
Pittsburgh, PA 15203
412-431-2489
City Theatre Company presents contemporary theatre at its South Side theater.

Pittsburgh Public Theater
Six Allegheny Square
Pittsburgh, PA 15212
412-321-9800
The Pittsburgh Public Theatre is a nationally recognized professional theater that presents contemporary drama, comedy, musicals, world classics and premieres of new works. The theater, currently housed on Pittsburgh's North Side, will be moving to a new downtown theater in 1999.

Jazz

Manchester Craftsmen's Guild Jazz Series
Manchester Craftsmen's Guild
1815 Metropolitan
Pittsburgh, PA 15233
412-322-0800
Year round jazz with world renowned artists in a state-of-the-art-facility on Pittsburgh's North Side.

Museums
Pittsburgh, Downtown-Northside

Carnegie Science Center
One Allegheny Avenue
Pittsburgh, PA 15212-5850
412-237-3400
This museum features exhibits for children and adults on science and the environment. Many displays are interactive. The Science Center also has a large-screen Omnimax theater and a World War II submarine. They have special educational programs for children.

The Andy Warhol Museum
117 Sandusky Street
Pittsburgh, PA 15212-5850
412-237-8300
This recently opened museum showcases the world's largest collection of Andy Warhol's art, as well as his films. Andy Warhol was born in Pittsburgh and attended Carnegie Technical University (now Carnegie Mellon University) before moving to New York. This is the most comprehensive single-artist museum in the world. Drawings, prints, painting, sculpture, film, audio/videotapes, and archives document the artist's life. Exhibits change regularly.

Fort Pitt Museum
101 Commonwealth Place
Pittsburgh, PA 15222
412-281-9284
The Fort Pitt Museum recalls the fierce struggle between France and Great Britain for Western Pennsylvania and the old Northwest, and tells the history of Fort Duquesne, Fort Pitt, and early Pittsburgh.

Senator John Heinz Pittsburgh Regional History Center
1212 Smallman Street
Pittsburgh, PA 15222
412-454-6000
The History Center is a great place to learn about Southwestern Pennsylvania's

history and cultures. It features special exhibits highlighting music, ethnic groups, and the culture of Pittsburgh's past. This is a must-see museum for understanding the people who made Pittsburgh great.

The Mattress Factory
500 Sampsonia Way
Pittsburgh, PA 15212-4444
412-231-3169
This contemporary art museum specializes in site-specific installation art. Its exhibits surprise viewers with variety. The museum also serves as a research and development lab for artists.

The National Aviary in Pittsburgh
Allegheny Commons West
Pittsburgh, PA 15212
412-323-7235
The National Aviary contains 450 of the most exotic species of live birds and plants. There are many special exhibits. The Aviary is closed on Christmas Day.

The Pittsburgh Children's Museum
10 Children's Way
Pittsburgh, PA 15212
412-322-5058
Pittsburgh Children's Museum has special hands-on exhibits and programs designed especially for children. Here they can try out a two-story climbing maze and meet some of the world's most famous puppets.

The Society for Contemporary Crafts
2100 Smallman St.
Pittsburgh, PA 15222
412-261-7003
This visual arts organization has a 26-year history of presenting nationally known artists who use traditional craft materials—ceramic, glass, wood, metal, and fiber—to create new art forms.

Trinity Cathedral and Burying Grounds
328 6th Avenue
Pittsburgh, PA 15222
412-232-6404
Trinity Cathedral, church of Stephen Foster, is Pittsburgh's first burial ground.
Docent tours are offered Sunday at 11:45 a.m. and by appointment.

Pittsburgh, Oakland, East End

Carnegie Museum of Art and **Carnegie Museum of Natural History**
4400 Forbes Avenue
Pittsburgh, PA 15213-4080
412-622-3131
These are Pittsburgh's oldest and most famous museums. The Museum of Art
contains a world-class collection of paintings, sculpture, and temporary art exhibits.
They also have a film series of foreign films. The Museum of Natural History has
exhibits on dinosaurs, animals from around the world, civilizations, and geology.
Both museums have extensive educational programs and lectures for children and
adults.

Center for American Music at the Stephen Foster Memorial
University of Pittsburgh
Pittsburgh, PA 15260
412-624-4100
This is a museum and library devoted to music in American life. It is the world
repository for materials related to Pittsburgh composer Stephen Collins Foster. The
Center charges a fee for guided tours.

Frick Art and Historical Center
7227 Reynolds Street
Pittsburgh, PA 15208-9701
412-371-0600
The Frick Art and Historical Center includes Clayton, the Victorian mansion built

by Henry Clay Frick, a carriage museum, and a separate museum that contains art collected by the Frick family. Clayton is a well preserved, restored example of how one of Pittsburgh's (and America's) wealthy industrial leaders lived and spent his money.

Heinz Memorial Chapel

University of Pittsburgh
Fifth and Bellfield Avenues
Pittsburgh, PA 15260
412-624-4157
This interfaith chapel is a prime example of adapted French Gothic architecture, made famous by the 23 stained-glass windows designed by Charles J. Connick. These are among the tallest windows in the world.

Hunt Institute For Botanical Documentation

Fifth Floor, Hunt Library
Carnegie Mellon University
Pittsburgh, PA 15260
412-268-2434
This is a research facility that presents an ongoing program of exhibitions to the public. The museum is largely devoted to botanical art and illustrations.

Nationality Classrooms, University of Pittsburgh

157 Cathedral of Learning
University of Pittsburgh
Pittsburgh, PA 15260
412-624-6000
Here is a unique exhibit of 24 classrooms, each designed to reflect the culture and style of a different country. They are styled from Byzantine, Romanesque, Baroque, Empire, Renaissance, and Folk motifs. Student guides offer daily tours for nominal fees. International gifts are available in a gift shop. For more than 50 years the Nationality Room committees have sponsored scholarships for students to study abroad. A special open house in December features traditional music, dance, and foods of some of the represented countries.

Phipps Conservatory
One Schenley Park
Pittsburgh, PA 15213-3830
412-622-6914
Phipps Conservatory is a large, Victorian glasshouse that displays plants from climates all over the world. Their spring flower show is especially popular.

Pittsburgh Center for the Arts
6300 Fifth Avenue
Mellon Park
Pittsburgh, PA 15232
412-361-0873
The Center for the Arts has exhibits of contemporary, regional, national, and international art, as well as art classes for adults and children.

Pittsburgh Zoo
One Hill Road
Pittsburgh, PA 15206-1178
412-665-364.
The Zoo has more than 4,000 animals, fish, birds, and reptiles from around the world. The recently remodeled zoo houses animals in environments designed to resemble the animals' natural habitats.

Rodef Shalom Biblical Botanical Gardens
4905 Fifth Avenue
Pittsburgh, PA 15206
412-621-6566
The gardens are open from June to mid-September, and present both plants mentioned in the Bible and those with Biblical names. The public can view more than 100 temperate and tropical species; this garden is the most complete and largest garden of its kind in the country.

Northwest

Harmony Museum
218 Mercer Street
Harmony, PA 16037
724-452-7341
The village of Harmony is a national landmark. In 1804, it became the first home of the Harmony Society. Most of the buildings here are open to the public and show periodic exhibitions, including those concerning Mennonites and Harmonists (1815) and the works of Charles Flowers, the well-regarded 19th-century gunsmith.

The Hoyt Institute of Fine Arts
124 East Leisure Avenue
New Castle, PA 16101
724-652-2882
An art museum and a period home, built in 1913, are on view here year round. There are monthly exhibitions and workshops involving the everyday life of the period.

Lawrence County Historical Society
408 N. Jefferson Street
New Castle, PA 16103
724-658-4022
This is a local history museum in a turn-of-the century mansion that features finely crafted woodwork and leaded bevelled glass. Tours are welcome.

Old Economy Village
1401 Church Street
Ambridge, PA 15003
724-266-4500
These seventeen restored buildings (1824-1830) represent the final home of the Harmony Society. They contain original Harmonist furniture, paintings, ceramics, scientific instruments and glass. The gardens, which reveal the group's appreciation for symmetrical forms, are some of the most beautiful in the region.

Zelienople Historical Society
243 S. Main Street
Zelienople, PA 16063
724-452-9457
Buhl House (1805) and Passavant House (1808), the homes of the city's founders, contain the historical society, a library, and artifacts. Tours are given May–October and by appointment. The society also does genealogical work.

Southwest

Duncan and Miller Glass Museum
525 Jefferson Avenue
Washington, PA 15301
724-225-9950
Opened in 1993 after 17 years at the Washington County Historical Society, the public can see fine pressed and blown glass manufactured by the Duncan Company (1872-1955) at this museum.

Meadowcroft Museum of Rural Life
401 Meadowcroft Road
Avella, PA 15312
724-587-3412
The 14,000-year-old history of the land now called Western Pennsylvania is revealed on this 200-acre multi-unit museum. Here the viewer can find exhibitions, tours, workshops, and hands-on programs.

Neville House
1375 Washington Pike
Bridgeville, PA 15017
412-279-3385
Visitors can view the home (c. 1785) of John Neville, friend of Washington and Lafayette, commander at Fort Pitt, and Revolutionary War hero. He was involved in the Whiskey Rebellion of 1794. Tours are given by appointment.

Pennsylvania Trolley Museum
1 Museum Road
Washington, PA 15301
724-228-9256
This is an operating trolley museum where visitors can ride into the park aboard one of Pennsylvania's historic streetcars. Trolley rides, guided tours, exhibitions, films, and a gift shop are all available.

Southeast

Bushy Run Battlefield
Route 993
Jeannette, PA 15644
724-527-5584
This site commemorates the conflict between British and Native American forces that allowed the opening of the Ohio frontier to European settlement in the eighteenth century. It is the only recognized Native American battlefield in Pennsylvania.

Fallingwater
Route 381, RD1
Mill Run, PA 15464
724-329-8501
Frank Lloyd Wright's Fallingwater is one of the world's most famous houses. Built in 1936 for Pittsburgh's Kaufmann family, it sits above a waterfall in the Laurel Highlands and still contains many of the original furnishings. You must call to make reservations to tour the house, illustrated on the opposite page.

Fort Ligonier
Routes 31 and 711
Westmoreland County
724-238-9701
Fort Ligonier is a constructed eighteenth-century fort of the French and Indian War period. The museum has an extensive collection of archeological objects and eighteenth-century art.

Photo courtesy of Western Pennsylvania Conservancy/Fallingwater.

Fort Necessity
National Battlefield
1 Washington Parkway
Farmington, PA 15437
724-329-5512
Here, on July 3, 1754, George Washington surrendered to the French and Native American forces that surrounded his fort. It was his first military foray, and the only surrender of his career. You will be surprised by the size of the building.

Friendship Hill National Historic Site
State Route 166
Point Marion, PA 15474
724-725-9190
Friendship Hill preserves the country estate of Albert Gallatin, Secretary of the Treasury under Presidents Thomas Jefferson and James Madison. He served his country for nearly seven decades. The museum is operated by the National Park Service.

Kentuck Knob
PO Box 305
Kentuck Road
Chalk Hill, PA 15421
724-329-1901
This is a newly restored Frank Lloyd Wright house recently opened to the public. It is located in the Laurel Highlands. Call for reservations. This architectural structure offers an interesting stylistic contrast to the low horizontal lines of Fallingwater.

West Overton Museums
West Overton Village
Scottdale, PA 15683
724-887-7910
Historians have recreated a nineteenth-century industrial village here: distillery, museum, Abraham Overholt homestead, birthplace of Pittsburgh industrialist Henry Clay Frick. The large barns are currently being restored. Tours are available, and there are special and seasonal events.

George Westinghouse Museum
Commerce Street
Wilmerding, PA 15148
724-825-3004
This museum has a fine collection of nineteenth-century antiques, including tableware and glassware, a full-size replica of the first Time Capsule, a recording of the world's first commercial radio broadcast, and an array of early home appliances.

Westmoreland Museum of American Art
221 N. Main St.
Greensburg, PA 15601
724-837-1500
With changing exhibitions and collections, this museum seeks to educate the public with its comprehensive collection of American art from the eighteenth century to the present.

Northeast

Butler County Historical Society Office
National City Bank Building
Corner of Main and Jefferson Streets
Butler, PA 16001
724-283-8116
Here are four historic sites: Cooper Cabin (1810), Shaw House (1828), Little Red Schoolhouse (1838), and the Butler County Heritage Center. Each tells a unique story of early country life. Group tours can be arranged.

Rachel Carson Museum
613 Marion Avenue
Springdale, PA 15144
724-274-5459
Explore the birthplace and childhood home of ecologist and author Rachel Carson (1907-1964), whose 1962 book *Silent Spring* helped launch the environmental movement. There are guided tours and classes.

Coolspring Power Museum
Main Street
Coolspring, PA 15730
814-849-6883
Over 115 years of industrial development are represented by a walk-through display
of more than 250 historically significant internal combustion engines.

Depreciation Lands Museum
4743 South Pioneer Road
Allison Park, PA 15101
412-486-0563
The museum represents a little-known corner of our historic past: the Depreciation
Lands. Learn about them at the Museum, Log House, Connestoga Wagon/
Tool Building, One-Room Schoolhouse, and Herb/Dye Garden.

Hartwood
215 Saxonburg Blvd.
Pittsburgh, PA 15238
412-767-9200
The equestrian estate of 629 acres has been restored, including a Tudor mansion,
fully furnished with English and American antiques, the stable complex, and the
gate lodge designed by Alfred Hopkins. Please make reservations for tours.

Sports

Civic Arena
Auditorium Place
Pittsburgh PA 15212
The Penguins play ice hockey January through March at the Civic Arena. You can
call 412-642-7367 for tickets. Known for the talented former player Mario
Lemieux, the Penguins are still a formidable team under the leadership of Jaromir
Jagr.

Three Rivers Stadium
400 Stadium Circle
Pittsburgh, PA 15212
Two of Pittsburgh's professional sports teams play at Three Rivers Stadium. The

Pirates play baseball from May to September. You can call 412-321-2827 for tickets or buy them just before the start of a game. The Steelers play American football from September though December. You can call 412-323-1200. It is fairly easy and inexpensive to see the Pirates play. The Steelers, however, are more difficult and expensive to watch because they are more popular and play fewer games. One reason for their popularity is their traditionally steady performance over the years. Pittsburgh, as you might have heard, is partial to football; many football greats are native to our suburbs, and a glance at the Steeler window decorations in even the most humble of neighborhoods reveals the heavy public identification with the local team.

The University of Pittsburgh (Pitt Panthers), **Carnegie Mellon University** (Tartans), and **Duquesne University** (The Dukes) have men's and women's sports teams (the teams are made up of students at the universities). Pitt's men's football and basketball teams receive national attention and games are often broadcast on television. The public can attend games. For schedule and ticket information call:

Carnegie Mellon University   412-268-3087
University of Pittsburgh   412-648-8300
Duquesne University   412-434-6565 (football), 434-5124 (basketball)

Parks and Recreation

Kennywood Park
4800 Kennywood Boulevard
West Mifflin, PA 15122
412-461-0500
Kennywood Park is one of the oldest amusement parks in the United States. It is famous for combining the best of old-style amusement parks such as wooden roller coasters, children's rides, and a Ferris Wheel with newer, faster rides such as the Steel Phantom.

Golf
Numerous golf courses abound in this area. Check the Yellow Pages for listings under "Golf Courses—Public."

Ohiopyle State Park
Westmoreland County
724-329-8591 (Park Office)
Ohiopyle Park is most famous for its excellent and challenging whitewater rafting on the Youghiogheny River. There are also camping facilities and extensive trails for walking, hiking, and bicycling.

Sandcastle
1000 Sandcastle Drive
West Homestead, PA 15120
412-461-1825
A great place for hot days in summer, Sandcastle has swimming pools and water slides and rides for children and adults.

Seven Springs Mountain Resort and Convention Center
1-800-452-2223

and

Hidden Valley Resort
1-800-443-8000
Both resorts are located in the Laurel Highlands southeast of Pittsburgh. In winter, these two resorts offer some of the best downhill skiing close to Pittsburgh. In summer, they have golf, hiking, tennis, and biking, among other activities. Check newspaper listings for other parks and recreation ideas.

Pittsburgh Festivals and Events

Seven Springs Winterfest, Late January to early February
This yearly festival, which takes place at one of the Pittsburgh area's best-known winter resorts, offers skiing, snowboarding, winter games, food, entertainment, and the well-attended Torchlight Parade.

Spring Flower Show: Phipps Conservatory, Mid-March to Mid-April
Phipps Conservatory in the city's Oakland section sponsors this annual event, which presents one of the most beautiful and comprehensive displays of exotic plants and flowers in the Tri-State area. Many Pittsburghers attend the show as a traditional rite of spring.

The UPMC Pittsburgh Marathon, Early May
Runners come from all over the world to participate in this exciting event. The course runs through the heart of the city and spectators are welcome to attend.

The Pittsburgh International Children's Festival, Mid-May
This event, which is offered every year at Allegheny Center/West Park, offers a wide variety of activities for children, including games, performances, rides, face painting, storytelling, and good food.

The Pittsburgh Folk Festival (Lawrence Convention Center), Late May
Pittsburgh is proud of its wide variety of ethnic traditions. This festival, one of the oldest in the city's history, celebrates diversity with music and dance troupe presentations, crafts, and traditional foods.

The Three Rivers Arts Festival (Point/Gateway/PPG/USX), June
This festival is an important June tradition in Pittsburgh. Pick up one of the free festival maps located throughout the city to locate particular attractions. Here, at selected sites, you will find juried exhibits of fine art, crafts such as gold and silver jewelry, woven and wooden goods, ceramics, art glass, and photographs. There are special programs for children. Concurrent musical performances—jazz, rock, classical—are also an important feature of the festival, as are the many types of food and refreshment.

The Pittsburgh Vintage Grand Prix (Schenley Park), Mid-July
The Vintage Grand Prix is run in Squirrel Hill's Schenley Park every year. The collection of classic racing cars that gather here for exhibition and competition is one of the largest in the country.

The Shadyside Arts Festival, August
On Walnut Street, you will see that the Shadyside Arts Festival, normally in August, features a wide selection of hand-crafted jewelry, pottery, and decorative objects. Artisans come from far and wide to participate, and the atmosphere is relaxed and family-oriented.

The Pittsburgh Three Rivers Regatta (Point Park), Early August
The Pittsburgh Regatta is a waterside event that celebrates the city's three rivers. With the area around the Point as a base, the Regatta offers the public a varied program of boat racing (including the humorous Anything that Floats Race), entertainment, food, and fun. The program often includes a parade and fireworks downtown, hot air ballons, and watercraft and aircraft shows.

Pittsburgh Sparkle Season, Light-Up Night, Fireworks (Point, PPG Plaza), Late November through December
The end-of-the year holiday season has been called "Sparkle Season" in Pittsburgh for several years. The first night of the season, during which downtown businesses leave their lights on in celebration, is called Light Up Night, the traditional inauguration of the shopping season in the heart of the city. Go to enjoy the lights and the holiday displays in department store windows. Attend the Celebrate the Season Parade, and visit the Neapolitan Tree Display at the Carnegie Museum of Art. Check your calendar and local television newscasts for many other holiday activities offered during Sparkle Season.

Guides to Pittsburgh and Western Pennsylvania

In addition to this one, there are many other resources of information about what the city has to offer: restaurants, entertainment, recreation in the city and state, art institutions, and special places. Many bookstores have a special section of books on Pittsburgh.

Greater Pittsburgh Metroguide is available in bookstores and at newsstands. This guide contains information for newcomers to the area as well as listings of stores and restaurants. Another resource is the *Guide to Living in Pittsburgh: A Narrative for New Pittsburghers* written by Brian K. Reid and Elaine A. Rich.

The *Pittsburgh Official Visitors Guide* from the Greater Pittsburgh Convention and Visitors Bureau also contains listings of local entertainment, event, and shopping opportunities. You can visit the **Visitors Bureau** downtown, on Mt. Washington, in Oakland, and at the airport to get free information about the city. Call 1-800-366-0093 to order a free information packet or request special information.

Pittsburgh Magazine publishes a monthly magazine that contains up-to-date listings of shopping, restaurants, and art events as well as articles on local issues and events. The magazine occasionally contains "best of" features that rank entertainment, shopping, restaurants, and events in the city. It is available in bookstores.

The **Greater Pittsburgh Museum Council** publishes a map of 50 museums in and around Pittsburgh. Look for the maps at the Visitors Bureau, or request a copy via mail by writing to the Greater Pittsburgh Museum Council, PO Box 7156, Pittsburgh, PA 15213.

Pittsburgh World Wide Web Resources

www.realpittsburgh.com
trfn.clpgh.org
www.pittsburgh.net
www.pittsburgh-cvb.org
www.pittsburghlive.com

Statistics

Pittsburgh World Firsts – By Event
The Pennsylvania Department, Carnegie Library of Pittsburgh

African-Americans: Derrick Bell – 1990
Derrick Bell, first African-American professor at Harvard University to receive tenure. Bell is a Pittsburgh native from the Hill district.
Source: *New Pittsburgh Courier*, 2 May 1990.

Air Pollution Disaster: Donora – 27 October 1948
Donora, Pennsylvania, was the first recorded air pollution disaster in the United States.
Source: *Morning Herald Standard*, 16 April 1970.

Aluminum-Faced Building: Alcoa – 1 August 1953
First aluminum-faced skyscraper was the Alcoa Building, a 30-story, 410 foot structure. Exterior walls were thin stamped aluminum panels.
Note: Company had previously built a 4 +-story administration building at Davenport, Iowa (1948).
Source: Aluminum Company of America, "Aluminum on the Skyline."

Atomic-Powered Electric Plant: Shippingport – December 1957
The world's first full-scale atomic-powered plant for production of electricity was opened at Shippingport, Pennsylvania, for the Duquesne Light Company.
Source: *Popular Science Monthly*, August 1958.

Banana Split: Latrobe – 1904
The banana split was invented by Dr. Strickler, a pharmacist, at Strickler's Drug Store in Latrobe, Pennsylvania.
Sources: *The Pittsburgh Press*, 5 September 1986, p. B1; *Undercover Club Newsletter*, August 1993, p. 4.

Big Mac: Uniontown – 1967
Created by M.J. "Jim" Delligatti at his Uniontown, Fayette County, McDonald's. Thereafter introduced "to three of his other McDonald's in Pittsburgh. After test

marketing, the item began appearing on every McDonald's menu nationwide by 1968."
Source: *The Tribune-Review*, 5 May 1993, p. B1.

Bingo – circa 1920s
Originated in Pittsburgh by Hugh J. Ward. Mr. Ward began running the game at carnivals in the early 1920s and took it nationwide in 1924. He secured a copyright on the game and wrote a book of Bingo rules in 1933.
Source: *Undercover Club Newsletter*, August 1993, p. 4.

Bridge, Wire Cable Suspension – May 1845
Marked the opening date of the first wire cable suspension aqueduct bridge in the world. Built by John Augustus Roebling, it spanned the Allegheny River at 11th Street. It had 7 spans of 160 feet each, consisting of a wooden trunk to hold water and supported by a continuous wire cable on each side 7 inches in diameter.
Source: *Bridges of Pittsburgh*, (qr917.4886 W63).

Carnegie Hero Fund Commission – 12 March 1904.
This date marked the establishment of the Hero Fund, for it was then that Andrew Carnegie transferred 5 million dollars in first collateral 5 percent bonds of the U.S. Steel Corporation. The by-laws were adopted 20 May 1904 in Pittsburgh. The first award was a bronze medal which was presented to Louis A. Bauman, Jr., 17, a laborer, who saved Charles Stevick, 16, also a laborer, from drowning (near Wilkinsburg, Pennsylvania).
Source: *Pittsburgh Sun Telegraph*, 27 February 1954.

Ferris Wheel: George W. Ferris – 1892/1893
The first Ferris Wheel was in operation at the World's Fair (Columbian Exposition) in Chicago. 264 feet high, more that 2,000 passengers at a load, it was invented by civil engineer, George Washington Gale Ferris (1859-1896), a native of Pittsburgh (204 Arch Street, North Side).
Sources: *The Pittsburgh Press*, 1 August 1954, p. 5;
The Pittsburgh Press, 19 April 1959;
Guide to the State Historical Markers of Pennsylvania, 1991, p. 130.

Gas Station: Gulf – 1 December 1913
Built by Gulf Refining Company at Baum Boulevard and St. Clair Street in East

Liberty. It was designed by J. H. Geisey.
Sources: Gulf Oil Corporation;
Pittsburgh Post-Gazette, 16 September 1980, p. 17.

Holiday, Saturday – 1 June 1881
First Saturday half holiday was inaugurated in U. S. by George Westinghouse, the inventor, who established the custom in his factory.
Source: *A Life of George Westinghouse*, (r92 W568p), p. 294-295.

Hospital, Federal – 1778
Hand Hospital opened. This was the first federal hospital built in America, and for 64 years was the only medical institution west of the Alleghenies. (While the city's first real hospital, Hand was not a general hospital.)
Source: *Pittsburgh's Fortresses of Health*, (r362.1P6744)

Industries: Air Brake – April 1869
In the first practical demonstration, an air brake train made a trip from Union Station in Pittsburgh to Steubenville.
Source: *George Westinghouse*, (r92 W568g), P. 73.

Industries: Aluminum – November 1888
World's first production of commercial aluminum. Aluminum was produced in commercial quantities on this date by the Pittsburgh Reduction Company (which later developed into the Aluminum Company of America). It was based upon the invention of Charles Martin Hall (patented 2 April 1889).
Sources: *Greater Pittsburgh*, November 1948, p. 21
The Pittsburgh Press, 5 October 1948.

Library, Carnegie: Allegheny – 13 February 1890
The Carnegie Library in Allegheny City, the first library given under the Carnegie formula, was opened to the public after being dedicated by President Benjamin Harrison. (Under the Carnegie formula, although Andrew Carnegie gave the building, the city had to agree to maintain the library). Design by Smithmeyer and Pelz, the Washington architectural firm that designed the Library of Congress.
Sources: *Typo-graphic*, January 1968;
Files of the Pennsylvania Department.

Library, Carnegie: Braddock – 30 March 1889
The Carnegie Library of Braddock, the first Carnegie Library in America, was dedicated. This was an endowed library. Carnegie Free Library of Allegheny was the first library given under the Carnegie formula, that is, Andrew Carnegie gave the building on the condition that the city maintain the library.
Source: *The Pittsburgh Press*, 31 March 1989.

Map, Road – Spring 1914
The first road map distributed by an oil company was a 1914 map of Allegheny County by Gulf Oil Corporation. 10,000 distributed to registered automobile owners at the suggestion of William Akin, an advertising man who prepared it.
Source: "Mileposts of Map Progress" by Bert O. Meadowcroft in Gulf Oil's *Orange Disc*.

Motion Picture Theater – 19 June 1905
The first theater in the world devoted exclusively to the exhibition of motion pictures was the "Nickelodeon," which was opened by Harry Davis in an empty store at 433-435 Smithfield Street, Pittsburgh, Pennsylvania. It had 96 seats taken from Davis' theaters. Among the first films were "Poor But Honest" and "The Baffled Burglar."
Source: *Allegheny County: A Sesquicentennial Review*, (r974.885 K17).

Petroleum Refining – circa 1850s
Samuel Kier experimented with the first known distilling process for petroleum. On Seventh Avenue, just East of the old Pennsylvania Canal near Grant Street, Kier established (1853 or 1854) the first successful petroleum refinery in the Western hemisphere.
Sources: *The Western Pennsylvania Historical Magazine*, v. 42, p. 356; *Pennsylvania Internal Affairs Bulletin*, June 1965.

Picturephone – 30 June 1970
At 9:40 a.m. Mayor Peter Flaherty made the world's first regular service Picturephone call to John D. Harpor of Alcoa.
Source: *The Pittsburgh Press*, 30 June 1970, p. 2.

Polio Vaccine – 26 March 1953
Dr. Jonas E. Salk, a 38-year-old University of Pittsburgh researcher and professor,

reported success of a new polio vaccine tried on human beings; the vaccine was developed by him and his staff at Pitt.
Source: *The Pittsburgh Press*, 12 April 1955.

Printing Press: Continuous Roll – 14 April 1863
This marked the date the patent was granted for the first printing press to use a continuous web or roll of paper. This was the Bullock Press, produced by William Bullock of Pittsburgh in 1865. It was the first machine built especially for curved stereotype plates. It printed both sides of the sheet and cut either before or after printings (U.S. patent #38,200.)
Source: *Famous First Facts*, 483.

Pull-Tab on Cans – 1962
Alcoa developed the pull-tab and Iron City Brewery was the first cannery to market it (1962); the first in the world to do so, for a long time, pull-tabs were only used in this area.
Sources: Iron City Brewery, 8 March 1995;
Pennsylvania Department files: Pittsburgh. Industries. Brewing.

Radio Broadcast: Church Service – 2 January 1921
The first church service broadcast in the world originated in the Calvary Protestant Episcopal Church (315 Shady Avenue, Pittsburgh) and was transmitted through the facilities of KDKA Radio.
Source: *A Traveler's Guide to Historic Western Pennsylvania*, p. 69.

Radio Broadcast, Commercial: KDKA – 2 November 1920
The world's first broadcast by a commercially licensed radio station was the Harding-Cox presidential election returns of November 2, 1920, on KDKA Radio, Pittsburgh. Thus, KDKA is the world's first commercial radio station.
Sources: *Undercover Club Newsletter*, August 1993, p. 4;
A Traveler's Guide to Historic Western Pennsylvania, p. 71.

Radio Broadcast: Phonograph Records – 17 October 1919
Broadcast of phonograph records on a regular schedule was begun by Frank Conrad from a brick garage in the rear of his house at 7750 Penn Avenue. (Licensed July 1916; canceled during World War I.)
Source: *A Traveler's Guide to Historic Western Pennsylvania*, p. 70.

Roof, Retractable: Civic Arena – 18 September 1961
Pittsburgh's Civic Arena is the world's first auditorium with a retractable roof. At the time, it was the world's largest opening and closing roof—three times the size of St. Peter's dome, the Vatican.
Source: *Greater Pittsburgh*, September 1961.

Sky Ballet – 16-18 April 1970
Otto Piene introduces sky ballet with balloons in downtown Pittsburgh.
Source: Pennsylvania Department files.

Sports: Baseball: World Series – 13 October 1903
The first of baseball's modern World Series ended before 7,455 persons at Boston. The Pittsburgh Pirates were defeated by Boston 4-3 and lost the Series 3 games to five. Games played in Pittsburgh on October 6,7,8 and 10.
Sources: *Pittsburgh Gazette*, 14 October 1903;
Official World Series Records from 1903-1975.

Steamboat: "New Orleans" – 20 October 1811
The "New Orleans", the first steamboat to navigate the Western waters, sailed for New Orleans. Didn't arrive at New Orleans until 10 January 1812. Began regular trips between Natchez and New Orleans on 23 January 1812. Launched 17 March 1811.
Sources: *The Pittsburgh Press*, 15 October 1961;
The Pittsburgh Press, 29 June 1930.

Submarine, Atomic: Engine – 21 January 1954
The U.S.S. Nautilus, the first atomic submarine, which was powered by an engine built by Westinghouse Electric Corporation, was launched at Groton, Connecticut.
Source: *Pittsburgh Sun-Telegraph*, 20 January 1954.

Telephone: International Communications Center – 28 November 1969
Pittsburgh became the first inland center for overseas telephone calls.
Source: *The Pittsburgh Press*, 28 November 1969.

Television Station, Educational – 1 April 1954
WQED, operated by the Metropolitan Pittsburgh Educational Station, went on the air. First community-sponsored educational television station in America. In 1955, it was the first to telecast classes to elementary schools.
Sources: WQED;
Guide to the State Historical Markers of Pennsylvania, 1991, p. 129;
Pennsylvania Department files.

Television Stations, Educational: Two – 16 July 1958
Pittsburgh was the first city to have two educational TV channels, when a second channel, WQEX, was granted.
Source: WQED-WQEX Public Relations Department.

Transplants – 3 December 1989
First heart, liver and kidney transplant done in simultaneous operations at Presbyterian-University Hospital.
Source: *The Pittsburgh Press* 4 December 1989, p. A1.

Unions, Labor: American Federation of Labor – 15-18 November 1881
The American Federation of Labor (A.F. of L.) held its first national convention at Pittsburgh.
Source: *Western Pennsylvania Historical Magazine*, v. 6.

University Skyscraper: Cathedral of Learning – 21 September 1926
Ground was broken for the University of Pittsburgh's Cathedral of Learning, the first university skyscraper.
Source: *Pittsburgh Gazette Times*, 22 September 1926.

Weather

Americans measure temperature in degrees Fahrenheit (F). You can convert Fahrenheit degrees into Celsius degrees by subtracting 32, multiplying by 5 and then dividing by 9. For example, 80° F is 26.7° C. Temperatures in the following paragraph are given in Fahrenheit degrees followed by Celsius degrees.

With an average year-round temperature of 59.9° F, Pittsburgh has four distinct seasons. Summer days (June through August) are humid and warm, often hot.

Temperatures can range from 50° (around 10° C) at night, to 80° (around 28° to 30° C) during the day. On hot days the temperature will rise above 90° (above 32° C). The warmest month is July, with an average high of 82.7° F. There are frequent thunder storms and sometimes dangerous lightening. In fall or autumn (September through November), temperatures are cooler and less humid. Temperatures range between 40° and 70° (5° to 21° C). Nights can be cool. Many people like fall because tree leaves change from green to red, orange, yellow, and brown. Winter (December through February) is cold, snowy (sometimes rainy), and gray. Temperatures range between 20° and 30° (-7° and 0° C). The coldest month is January, with an average temperature of 34.2° F. It snows frequently in the winter and streets and sidewalks are often icy. On the worst snow days, schools close for the day (school snow days are announced on the radio or on TV). Spring weather (March through May) can be unpredictable. Temperatures range from 30° to 60° (-1° to 16° C). In March and April, combinations of rain, snow, and freezing temperatures can be followed by sunny, warm, clear days. It rains frequently in May and June.

Pittsburgh Weather

Average days per year that are:

Clear	59
Partly cloudy	105
Cloudy	203
Rainy	153
Snowy	13

Average accumulations:

Rain	37 inches
Snow	40 inches

Population (1997)

State of Pennsylvania: 12,056,112
Southwestern Pennsylvania: 4,750,000
Allegheny County: 1,323,700
City of Pittsburgh: 369,879
Median Age: 36

Crime

According to the Allegheny County Department of Economic Development, Pittsburgh's crime rate compares favorably to that of other comparably sized cities:

Crime Index Total

Pittsburgh, PA   393.4

Cincinnati, OH	573.6
Buffalo, NY	754.8
Washington, D.C.	771.4
Columbus, OH	682.3
Baltimore, MD	1356.1
New York, NY	1865.5

Housing

The National Association of Realtors provides the following statistics on the affordability of the city's housing (based on median sale price for a single family home, first quarter 1996):

Median Purchase Price (U.S. Dollars)

Pittsburgh	$ 84,000
Columbus, OH	$ 107,000
Philadelphia, PA	$ 118,000
Washington D.C.	$ 155,000
New York, NY	$ 169,000
Boston, MA	$ 177,000

Sales Tax

Excluding food and clothing:
7% in Allegheny County
6% in surrounding counties

Transportation

Airways

Pittsburgh has the second busiest airport in America, the Greater Pittsburgh International Airport, which was built in 1992.

Highways

According to the Allegheny County Department of Economic Development (1997), Pittsburgh is centrally located next to the following highways:

Interstate I-79 (North/South)
Interstate I-279 (North/West)

Interstate I-376 (East/West)
Interstate I-76 (Turnpike)

Waterways
Pittsburgh is the largest inland port in the nation

30 ft. deep maximum
40 public terminals
12 regional carriers, 5 long-haul carriers
17 locks and dams
50 million tons of cargo annually

Railways
CSX, Conrail, Wheeling, and Lake Erie

Market Access
According to the Allegheny County Department of Economic Development, Pittsburgh and its surrounding areas have market access to Toronto, Washington D.C., Philadelphia, Baltimore, New York, Boston, Detroit, Chicago, Atlanta, and St. Louis. The city has access to 51% of the U.S. population, 50% of the Canadian population, and 53% of the U.S. buying income.

NOTES

To order additional copies of

Understanding Pittsburgh:
A Guide for International Visitors and Residents,

please call the Pittsburgh Council for International Visitors
at
(412) 624-7800

or contact our office by e-mail at

pciv@pitt.edu